D1293554

An Ordinary Life
Lived in an Extraordinary Way

REFLECTIVE READINGS

REFLECTIVE READINGS

An Ordinary Life
Lived in an Extraordinary Way

Blessed Mary Angela Truszkowska

A Translation
by
Sister Mary Clarentine Dzienis, CSSF
Sister Mary Emelita Makowski, CSSF

From the original *Rekolekcje z . . .*
Błogosławiona Maria Angela Truszkowska
by
Reverend Jan D. Szczurek

Felician Sisters
Presentation of the Blessed Virgin Mary Province
Livonia, Michigan
2005

Originally published in Polish as *Rekolekcje z . . . Błogosławiona Maria Angela Truszkowska*

© 2002 by Wydawnictwo „M", Kraków

Published by Wydawnictwo „M"
ul. Zamkowa 4/4, 30-301 Kraków
Printed by Pracownia AA, Pl. Na Grobłach 5, Kraków

English translation: *An Ordinary Life Lived in an Extraordinary Way*

© 2005 by The Felician Sisters, OSF, Livonia, Michigan
  All rights reserved.

Editor: Sister Mary Cynthia Strzalkowski, CSSF

Technical Editor and Cover Design:
    Sister Mary Francis Lewandowski, CSSF

ISBN 0-9771905-0-1

Published by: Felician Sisters
          36800 Schoolcraft Road
          Livonia, Michigan 48150

Printed and bound in the United States of America
by Kimcraft Printers, Inc., Canton, Michigan

CONTENTS

ABBREVIATIONS

AA   *"Apostolicam actuositatem"*, *Decree on the Apostolate of Lay People*, Vatican Council II.

Archives   Information acquired from the Archives of the Felician Sisters on Smolensk Street in Krakow.

CCC   *Catechism of the Catholic Church*, Liguori, 1994, (arabic numerals identify the paragraphs).

FBP   *Felician Book of Prayers*, Canton, 2001.

GS   *"Gaudium et spes"*, *Pastoral Constitution on the Church in the Modern World*, Vatican Council II.

LG   *"Lumen gentium"*, *Dogmatic Constitution on the Church*, Vatican Council II.

Modl.   *Modlitewnik felicjanski*, Rome, 1982.

NMI   *"Novo millennio ineunte"*, *At the Beginning of the New Millennium*, John Paul II, 2001.

SW   *Selected Writings* of Mary Angela Truszkowska, New York, 1977-1984, Volumes I-III, (roman numerals indicate the volume; arabic numerals, the page).

Writings   *Writings* of St. Francis of Assisi, *Omnibus of Sources*, Chicago, 1973, (roman numerals indicate the part; arabic numerals, the page).

PREFACE

We are accustomed to naming someone a spiritual father. But it is a rare occurrence to name someone a spiritual mother. This title of spiritual mother, however, is readily given to Blessed Mary Angela who gave spiritual birth to a religious community, the Felician Sisters. Blessed Mary Angela Truszkowska is the Foundress of the Congregation of the Sisters of St. Felix of Cantalice whose one hundred and fiftieth anniversary is celebrated in 2005. The spiritual legacy of the Blessed Foundress is a treasure which by her beatification in 1993 became the possession of the entire Church. Therefore, any member of the Church, not only can, but should benefit from the spiritual wealth of Mother Mary Angela.

Mary Angela is her religious name. She was born on 16 May 1825 in Kalisz, Poland. At her baptism on 1 January 1826 in the famous collegiate church of St. Joseph in Kalisz, she received the name Sophia Camille. Her parents, landed gentry, were Joseph and Josephine (Rudzinska) Truszkowski. Sophia Camille was the eldest of the seven children in the family. Her parents were solicitous for her to have a good upbringing, especially a solid education. As a child Sophia Camille gave evidence of sensitivity for the poor and, almost on every occasion in walks in the city, she gave alms from her personal savings whenever she met someone in need. Anastasia Kotowicz, the daughter of her godmother, had a great influence on her spiritual formation. Sophia Camille was a diligent student with an inquiring mind and it was even said of her that she was greedy for knowledge and learning. She was acknowledged for her scholarship both by her teachers and school companions.

Unfortunately, at the age of 16 Sophia Camille was diagnosed with respiratory problems. To regain her strength and health she traveled to Switzerland with Anastasia as her companion. There, surrounded by the beauties of nature and attentive to the voice of God in her heart and soul, she fell in love with prayer. Perhaps it was then that she began thinking about devoting her life to the exclusive service of God. After more than a year, young Sophia Camille returned to her family home, where she completed her education by availing herself of her father's vast library collection of books. She studied the French language which she subsequently taught to her younger siblings. Her sister Hedwig wrote in her memoirs that, even as a child, Sophia Camille prayed frequently, was genuinely pious, and rose early each morning to run to church (Archives).

It was on 14 June 1848 that, following an experience of an extraordinary meeting with God, Sophia Camille decided to enter the convent of the Visitation Sisters. This never actualized due to the illness of her father. As his nurse, she traveled with him to a health resort in Salzbrunn. When her father's treatment was completed, they visited Cologne. While at prayer in the city's cathedral, God gave Sophia Camille a clear sign that her place is not in a cloistered convent. She still did not know what God really expected of her. On the trip back to Warszawa, they detoured to Krakow— a city which greatly impressed Sophia Camille. Her love for Poland was intensified by this opportunity to visit the site of so much history of her country. Through this journey the Lord prepared her for future undertakings.

After her return to Warszawa, she dedicated herself to charitable works and perfecting her interior life. Her confessor and spiritual director, Father Augustine Brzezkiewicz, predicted that she would found a religious community. By 1851, with the permission of her parents, Sophia Camille took care of orphaned children in whichever way she could.

When in 1854 the Society of St. Vincent de Paul of the Merciful Christ was organized in the Holy Cross Parish, Sophia Camille joined in its activities as one of the first members. It was then that she oriented herself to the fact that giving a piece of bread to a poor child is not adequate; the child's soul also needs care.

During the same year Sophia Camille gathered together a few homeless orphaned children and a few elderly women who had no roofs over their heads. She housed them in two rooms in the attic of a building in Warszawa. This was the beginning of the *Shelter* which later was to be known as the *Institute of St. Felix of Cantalice*. She entrusted her *Shelter* to the care of St. Felix, a Capuchin Brother, who died in 1587 and before whose altar, located in the Capuchin Church on Miodowa Street in Warszawa, she prayed frequently.

Her undertaking inspired many benevolent persons, among whom were included the Countess Gabriela (Brezow) Wrotnowska and Clothilde Ciechanowska, Sophia Camille's cousin and sincere friend. In 1854, following the advice of Father Augustine, she chose a Capuchin, Father Honorat Kozminski, for a confessor.

Father Benjamin Szymanski, the then Capuchin Provincial Superior, had unsuccessfully attempted to import a Franciscan Religious Community of Nursing Sisters from Munster, Germany. It was his plan that these sisters were to have conducted a renewal of the religious spirit among the laity, but in place of the sisters, he appointed the young Father Honorat to revive the activities of the Franciscan Secular Third Order. His fervent sermons attracted many, among them also Sophia and Clothilde. In May of 1855 they joined the Third Order of St. Francis and received their religious names: Sophia—Sister Angela, and Clothilde —Sister Veronica.

In July of that year they began living together with those poor who were their charges. On 21 November 1855 on the feast of the Presentation of the Blessed

Virgin Mary, before the icon of the Mother of God of Czestochowa, they dedicated themselves to God and the service of their neighbor. It is this date that the Felician Sisters consider the date of the founding of their Congregation, with the Mother of God of Czestochowa as the actual Foundress.

A tremendous support for Sophia Truszkowska was the solicitude of Father Benjamin over this enterprise. It was he who oversaw the possibilities of bypassing the czar's various regulations and proscriptions which curtailed the activities of all religious. On Good Friday, 10 April 1857, ten tertiaries were invested in a religious habit. That very day, undoubtedly through the intervention of Father Benjamin, Archbishop Fijalkowski came to the sisters to give them his blessing. These events significantly contributed to the initial development of the Congregation. In 1856 Father Benjamin appointed Father Honorat as the director of the Congregation of the Felician Sisters. Mary Angela (Sophia Truszkowska) together with Father Honorat prepared an outlined plan for a religious community of women in the tradition of the spirituality of St. Francis of Assisi. Their life was to combine contemplation with apostolic ministry. A very important occurrence for the further development of the Congregation was the acceptance in 1859 of an invitation offered by the Agricultural Society for the sisters to assume ministerial responsibilities in the Centers of the villages.

According to an original plan, the Congregation was to consist of two groups of sisters: cloistered and active. In 1860 several of the sisters began leading a strictly contemplative life, while the remainder were to continue in apostolic ministry. However, in retaliation for aiding the Polish insurgents in 1863, by an order of suppression in 1864, all local homes of the Felician Sisters in the Polish Kingdom were to be closed. The cloistered Felician Sisters were escorted by convoy to the convent of the Bernardine Sisters in Lowicz. By the decision of Father Honorat, Mother Foundress joined them a few days later and remained there with the cloistered Felician Sisters until May of 1866. In time, this cloistered group severed its relationship with the Felician Sisters and by 1871 became independent. Today they are an enclosed community identified as Capuchin Poor Clares.

Fortunately, the above 1864 order of the czar did not affect the local homes of the Felician Sisters in Krakow which were under the Austrian rule. It became the nucleus of the Congregation in the Galicja region and from there the sisters were able to grow in number and expand their ministerial services.

Following the recognition of the Congregation by the Ministry of Vienna on 1 November 1865, Mary Angela in consultation with Father Honorat sent two sisters to Krakow with the assignment to prepare everything for the arrival of the Felician Sisters who had been dispersed after the suppression. A year later on 17 May 1866, Mary Angela also arrived and took up residence on Mikolajska Street. The next day, the first investiture of the novices took place in Krakow together with the vow ceremony during which the sisters pronounced their vows into the hands of the Mother Foundress. In a very short time there were many new local homes of Felician Sisters in this section of Poland under the Austrian domination.

Today, the Congregation of the Felician Sisters no longer has cloistered sisters, but the contemplative aspect of their spirituality is evident in the participation of the sisters in the daily adoration of the Most Blessed Sacrament in the Provincial Houses of the Congregation. In this way, and in imitation of their Mother Foundress, the sisters prayerfully support those sisters who are involved in apostolic ministry.

Mary Angela's rich spiritual life is worthy of special notice. The example of her life is an edifying lesson for all who are in pursuit of evangelical perfection. The proposed *Reflective Readings* present several features of her spiritual life which may become models for personal imitation.

The *Reflective Readings* are based on the *Selected Writings* of Mary Angela Truszkowska. From these writings a complete picture of Mother's spirituality cannot be created because these are the only letters which have been published. However, additional letters to the sisters as well as to Father Honorat were written by Mother Foundress.

The counseling that Mother offered solely by word-of-mouth survived only as personal memoirs and obviously all has not been recorded. More information can be found in the memoirs which have not as yet been published. These are available in the archives of the Congregation of the Felician Sisters. Some of these have been used as references in the reflections.

I wish to take this opportunity to express my sincere gratitude to the Felician Sisters of the Immaculate Heart of Mary Province in Krakow for their prayerful support and valued assistance which they rendered me while I wrote these meditative reflections. It was their kindness which prompted me to write this book. May they be granted many graces through the intercession of Blessed Mary Angela.

The prayers accompanying each reflection were selected from the *Modlitewnik felicjanski* or from the *Selected Writings* of Mother Mary Angela. The litany invocations are from the *Litany of Blessed Mary Angela Truszkowska, Foundress of the Congregation of the Sisters of St. Felix of Cantalice and Patroness of the Sick*. It is recited on the tenth of each month following the Mass of Petition and Thanksgiving at the relics of Blessed Mary Angela in the church of the Felician Sisters on Smolensk Street in Krakow. Prior to this recitation, there is a reading of all the petitions and thanksgivings for favors received through the intercession of Blessed Mary Angela. The tenth day of the month is a remembrance of the day of her death, 10 October 1899.

Reverend Jan D. Szczurek
Author
Krakow, 2002

EDITOR'S INTRODUCTION

The translation of this work by Reverend Jan D. Szczurek, originally published under the title, Blogoslawiona Maria Angela Truszkowska, was undertaken in anticipation of the 150th Anniversary of the Foundation of the Congregation of the Sisters of St. Felix of Cantalice.

Reverend Szczurek's book reflects an inspirational and candid approach to the highlights of the spiritual journey of Blessed Mary Angela, Foundress of the Felician Sisters. In preparing *An Ordinary Life Lived in an Extraordinary Way*, the translators—Sister Mary Clarentine Dzienis and Sister Mary Emelita Makowski—recognized the author's insightful use of the *Selected Writings* of our Foundress in his presentation of the many aspects of her deep Christian life lived in the Franciscan tradition and in faithfulness to God's will.

On this 150th Anniversary of the our Foundation, *An Ordinary Life Lived in an Extraordinary Way* is offered to our Felician Sisters as an opportunity to make a renewed personal contact with the treasures of the profound spirituality of our Blessed Foundress. Likewise, *An Ordinary Life Lived in an Extraordinary Way*, is offered to any sincerely inquiring Christian who is seeking to find the deeper meaning of life in an encounter with Christ in the company of a spiritual directress, Blessed Mary Angela.

Sister Mary Cynthia Strzalkowski, CSSF
Livonia, 2005

I

LOVE OF GOD

God is our Father and that is why he tells us to call him that in prayer. What should we fear having such a Father without whose will even one hair will not fall? It is surprising, that having such a Father, we could worry about anything else but that we should love him perfectly and serve him faithfully (SW III, 122).

To love God, above all, is the greatest commandment: "You should love the Lord your God with all your heart, with all your soul, with all your mind, and with all your strength . . . There is no greater commandment . . ." (Mk 12:30-31). Mother Mary Angela was well aware of this commandment. She knew that such was the will of God and desired with all her strength to realize it in a most perfect way by fixing her gaze incessantly upon her Master and Spouse, and by deepening that love unceasingly. She wrote to Sister Mary Bogdana, "Holy desires are like wings which transport the soul to heaven" (SW III, 110).

Does there exist anything more beautiful than the love of God? The Lord Jesus taught us and by example showed us how we should love God, his Father and ours. At the Last Supper while bidding his disciples farewell, he affirmed: "The world must know that I love the Father and do as the Father has commanded me" (Jn 14:31). Obedient to the will of the Father, he did not retreat from the painful torment of the cross. On the cross he demonstrated the power of that love and its dramatic effect, "for love is strong as death" (Sg 8:6). It was on the cross that Jesus revealed his submission to the Father to the highest degree, and

1

his love for humanity. In complete abandonment and the apparent silence of the Father, and rejected with utmost scorn, Jesus still forgives and embraces us (*cf.* Lk 23:28). In this way he teaches us: "There is no greater love than this: to lay down one's life for one's friends" (Jn 15:13).

The ideal of this love of God was incarnated in the life of St. Francis of Assisi. He named the virtue of love, *Lady of Holy Love*, linking it with holy obedience. In the *Praises of the Virtues* he explained that "holy love puts to shame all the temptations of the devil and the flesh and all natural fear" (Writings III, 133). He always remembered the words of the Apostle: "God is love and he who abides in love, abides in God, and God in him" (1 Jn 4:16). Undoubtedly he grieved over the fact that Love is not loved. In the *Praises of God*, he prayed: "You are Three in One . . . You are love" (Writings I, 125). In the *Sixth Admonition*, he wrote that he was deeply ashamed whenever he recalled the cruel suffering of the Lord, or the persecution of the saints who followed the Good Shepherd, while he and his brothers expected glory and honor for merely relating this (*cf.* Writings I, 81).

Mother Mary Angela did not limit herself to "relating" about the love of Christ and his saints. She did not have the occasion to shed her blood, because martyrdom was not her vocation. Still, she was bound to the cross of Christ with her whole heart and was willing to bear it to her last breath. She wished to respond to his love of neighbor with the most ardent love. That is why it was precisely in his cross that she perceived her deepest union with her Lord and Master.

In the *Spiritual Counsels* she wrote: "Let us love our Lord Jesus Christ, but let us love him on the cross because his heart is overjoyed when he finds love, pain, and silence in one and the same heart. What does it matter from what kind of wood our cross is hewed out as long as it is a cross to which love keeps us nailed" (SW III, 110).

If we would observe the events of the life of Mary Angela more closely, it would become very clear how the wood of her cross kept changing and how various were her trials and sufferings which she bore ever so patiently. In a particular way her patience was especially manifested in bearing the disability of deafness for almost thirty years!

From the depths of her heart, she desired that her spiritual daughters would love the crucified Savior without bounds. She hoped that they would persevere in this love of God, irrespective of spiritual consolations which would ease the bearing of the cross. She zealously urged Sister Mary Hedwig: "Show yourself worthy of his trust, prove that you are worthy to be called Spouse of the Crucified. Let love and not compulsion or need stretch and hold you on the cross—not the love which manifests itself in consolations, in tears, in elation, and in visions, but in perfect and willing fulfillment of God's will" (SW I, 106). This is truly a magnificent encouragement to a total disinterested love of God. This is what it means to love God above everything and not only for that which he provides.

The truth about God's love for us and our love for God is the most valuable of truths proclaimed by the Church. We owe our being to love—as the *Catechism of the Catholic Church* teaches—God "created man out of love, also calls him to love, which is the basic and innate vocation of every human being" (CCC 1604). Realizing this innate vocation, a person "reproduces" in himself the image and likeness of God (*cf.* Gn 1:27) who is Love himself (*cf.* 1 Jn 4:8-16). God "manifested his love to us through Christ's death for us while we still were sinners" (Rom 5:8). Thus it was not only in creation, but above all in the coming of the Son of God into the world that he revealed to us the inconceivable love of the One God in the Holy Trinity.

One can sin against God's love in various ways. The *Catechism of the Catholic Church* enumerates them as indifference, ingratitude, lukewarmness, acedia, and hatred of God. Indifference neglects or refuses to reflect on divine charity; it fails to consider its prevenient goodness and denies its power. Ingratitude fails or refuses to acknowledge divine charity and to return to him love for love. Lukewarmness is hesitation or negligence in responding to divine love; it can imply refusal to give oneself over to the prompting of charity. Acedia or spiritual sloth goes so far as to refuse the joy that comes from God and to be repelled by divine goodness. Hatred of God comes from pride. It is contrary to love of God whose goodness it denies, and whom it presumes to curse as the one who forbids sins and inflicts punishments (*cf.* CCC 2094).

Mother Angela not only deepened her love by avoiding even a shadow of imperfection, but through her mortifications desired to atone for sins against the love of God, especially the hatred of God by unreasonable persons. Not content with her personal mortifications, she counseled that reparation remain the enduring element of the spiritual life of the sisters. When perpetual adoration of the Blessed Sacrament became a possibility, she tried to convince the sisters to accept this service of nightly adoration for these reasons: first, that the Church is in great need; second, that the sisters of the Congregation are obligated to a sacrificial life; and third, it is necessary to plead for God's mercy upon souls threatened with eternal condemnation (*cf.* SW 1, 47). In a letter to Sister Mary Joseph, she explained to her that the reason for this great suffering which she was then enduring was because, in a matter of great importance, she had offered herself "to Jesus to atone for the offenses committed against him, and because these insults, especially at the present time, are so enormous, the reparation for them must also be great" (SW I, 158).

The ardent love of Mother Mary Angela for God is a perfect example for contemporary persons who do not perceive nor understand this love. Vatican Council II teaches that if a person exists "it is because God has created him through love, and through love continues to hold him in existence. A person cannot live fully according to truth, unless he freely acknowledges that love and entrusts himself to the Creator" (LG 19). Our Blessed Angela acknowledged this love early in her childhood and lived her life in accordance with this truth. In this way her life confirms that the teaching of the Church about the love of human beings for God can be fully realized. If it could be realized then, so can it be now.

The most beautiful and most authoritative witness of the love of Mother Mary Angela for God was given by John Paul II in the beatification homily when he reminded the listeners how she understood love: "Her greatest desire was to 'be consumed by love.' She understood that love is always an unselfish gift of self. 'To love is to give. Give everything that love demands. Give eagerly, without regret, with joy, with a desire that even more would be demanded.' These are her words, in which she concisely expressed her whole life program. She enkindled this love in the hearts of the sisters of her Congregation. This love is constantly the living ferment of the ministerial services, in which the Felician Sisters serve the Church in her native Poland and beyond its boundaries" (*Homily*, 18 April 1993).

Mother Mary Angela awakened this love of God in the hearts of her sisters effectively and firmly. To this day the sisters reflect this love with eyes fixed on the example of their Foundress. To be ever mindful of this, the Felician Sisters state in their *Constitutions*: "Her boundless love of God manifested itself in her complete surrender to his divine will and overflowed into compassion and mercy, consuming her in service to the needy and concern for the salvation of all people" (*Constitutions*, I).

Such a charism is a gift of the Holy Spirit. This same Spirit calls new vocations and strengthens the sisters in the realization of the charism of their Foundress. The contemporary world is in great need of this witness to the love of God, because today's civilization is "excessively entangled [. . .] in worldly affairs which may often impede its approach to God" (GS, 19).

PRAYER

Blessed Mary Angela, Foundress of the Congregation of the Felician Sisters
    – pray for us.
Prudent virgin, born in Poland
    – pray for us.
Given to penance for the sins of neighbor and the world
    – pray for us.

God our Father, you graced Blessed Mary Angela with a living faith and boundless love which she manifested in complete surrender to your divine will. By her prayers and witness may we strive to seek, to accept, and to fulfill your will in all circumstances of our lives (Oration from the Mass of Blessed Mary Angela).

II

LOVE OF NEIGHBOR

May Jesus support you in your work and dedication to those people. I can't tell you what a joy it is for me to see in you such a desire to save souls, for this is the best and undeniable evidence that you love God; for Holy Scripture tells us that he who says he loves God but does not love his neighbor is a liar, and our Lord says: "By their fruits you will know them" (SW I, 106).

The commandment of love of neighbor was for Mother Angela inseparably connected with the commandment of love of God. Such thinking is totally in accord with the Gospel and is the constant teaching of the Church. To love God and neighbor is by far of greater value than all the holocausts and sacrifices (*cf.* Mk 12:33).

Love of neighbor encompasses all the moral responsibilities because the fulfillment of this law of Christ is based on the fact that we bear each others' burdens. (*cf.* Gal 6:2). Its source is God, for it is the action of the Holy Spirit in us: "The love of God has been poured out in our hearts through the Holy Spirit who has been given to us" (Rom 5:5). Thanks to this, that same love animates our closeness to Jesus and our kindness to those closest to us who are our neighbors. Our Lord very clearly said: "As often as you did it for one of my least brothers, you did it for me" (Mt 25:40).

This oneness of the love of God and love of neighbor is also underlined in a letter by St. John: "The commandment we have from him is this: whoever loves God must also love his brother" (1 Jn 4:21).

The motive thereof is obvious. We are to love our neighbors because God loves them and gives all of them life (*cf.* 1 Jn 5:1). St James clarifies what is the practical realization of this commandment: "So it is with faith that does nothing in practice. It is thoroughly lifeless" (Jas 2:17). True love of neighbor does not depend on frequent verbal assurances of it, but on the concrete acts of help to those who are in need (*cf.* 1 Jn 3:18).

Christian love of neighbor differs from philanthropy which is the result of natural goodness and of a feeling of solidarity with other people. The difference here is grounded on the fact that love of neighbor has religious motivation and by its essence is a religious stance. It is a conscious and free response of a human being to God's love and is thus motivated more deeply and powerfully.

Love of neighbor lies at the very center of the spirituality of St. Francis of Assisi. He was totally convinced that love is the source of other virtues, above all of the fear of God and wisdom. He reminds the brothers of this in his *Admonitions* (*cf.* Writings I, 86) and in the *Testament of Siena* in the very first three lines he obligates them to always love each other. As he expounds on the theme of the *Our Father*, he makes it clear that to love a neighbor means to draw him closer to the love of God, to rejoice in his gifts, to sorrow with him in his misfortunes, and to be on guard to never scandalize anyone (*cf.* Writings I, 160). In his *Letter to All the Faithful*, he warns them that who cannot love his neighbor as himself should at least do no harm to him (*cf.* Writings II, 95).

St. Francis made the very foundation of his Order, the love of neighbor which he lived and which he taught his brothers to live. In the very beginning of the first chapter of his *Rule* he laid stress on the fact that this consists in "following the teachings and the footsteps of our Lord Jesus Christ" (Writings I, 31). In directing his brothers, he emphasized especially love of the enemy. In Chapter 22 of his *Rule*, he reminded them that it was Jesus Christ himself who gave the command about loving the enemy, and he himself gave us an example of this in his treatment of the traitor, and also of those who crucified him (*cf.* Mt 26:50). Love indeed was for St. Francis the *Holy Lady* who controlled all his life.

Mother Mary Angela was drawn to the example of St. Francis in a remarkable way. She wanted to imitate the Poverello in everything especially in his love of others, particularly the poor. She encouraged the sisters to be concerned about strengthening the spirit of St. Francis in the Congregation, so that by his example they would strive to work for the salvation of others (*cf.* SW I, 89, 161). She advised Sister Mary Cajetan to live in such a way that her whole life radiates "his humility, contempt of the world, poverty, and his love of God and neighbor" (SW III, 135).

In community life there are many occasions for showing love. So that a community can function normally, one or another member may have to exercise more self-control. These persons are occasions for others to practice mutual love. Mother Mary Angela was very well aware of this. Therefore, in her letter to Sister Mary Aniela she gave this wise advice about bearing with the imperfections of another sister: "[. . .] what can we do since it is not in our power to change someone; we must rather accept the person as she is, being mindful that Holy Scripture recommends that we bear one another's burdens, and that therein lies our merit and proof of our profound spirituality" (SW I, 37).

This advice is also evidence of Mother's very realistic outlook on life. It proved that she looked at community life as a place for perfecting mutual love even for the sisters who initially are a source of trouble to others.

An extremely precious value to common life is the possibility of recognizing one's own faults and imperfections. In a letter to Sister Mary Aniela, Mary Angela writes: "The common life is very difficult, but also most beneficial, for the life shows us what we are, what we lack, and what virtues we must practice" (SW I, 31).

The so-called "ochrony" [Editor's note: Polish translation for "Centers"] conducted by the new Congregation were an extremely clear-cut form for the realization of this love for others, especially the suffering and the poor. It was an undertaking consisting, to an extent, of the regular gathering of a group of children, youth, or adults for educational purposes. In the Centers the sisters conducted daily classes in prayer, catechism, reading, and writing for the little children. The same procedure was followed with the youth and adults. For the adults, however, meetings were generally scheduled for Sundays so as not to create difficulty for them in their daily work, and this especially for the farmers—if such Centers were organized in their villages. On other days of the week, meetings were held in the evenings, but Mother cautioned the sisters not to prolong them into late night hours (*cf.* SW III, 171). After evening devotions and with the consent of the pastors, the sisters frequently met with the parishioners for informative reading sessions. Mother Angela exhorted the sisters to work diligently in the Centers and to be solicitous about the organization of these Centers. She was also concerned about the adequate preparation of the sisters for this work. In 1862, in her *Directives to the Congregation* she strongly advised that "there be one sister who will give lectures in classroom theory on how to teach at the Centers and that the same theory should be taught at each Center" (SW III, 171).

It is of worth to make a comment on the Polish word "ochrony" [Editor's note: the Polish translation for "Centers"] which is the name of the ministerial undertakings which have been discussed above. The word means protection or preservation. Protection from what? Mother's instructions and the various activities in the Centers indicate that it is easy to deduce that it is protection from every kind of deprivation: material, intellectual, moral, and spiritual. For that reason the sisters taught them everything that could be useful, for example, handwork. In those days when many of the people lived in abject misery with no means for education, when the Catholic Church had no freedom for action, and when the Poles had to fight to keep their identity, the activities at the Centers were like a balsam for human wounds. Actually, these Centers saved the poor from illiteracy, from the degradation of their human dignity, from loss of hope, and above all from the danger of loss of eternal life because of prevalent immorality. It can be said that the Centers preserved human dignity in all its dimensions. The sisters were serving God in human beings: to serve a neighbor was to serve Christ.

A note, dated 1856 and written by an important government official, is found in the Archives among the early documents related to the *Institute of St. Felix*. It confirms the commitment of Mary Angela and her cousin, Mary Veronica, to the work for the poor. The author of the note wrote: "During the last bitter winter caused by extremely high costs of all commodities, sicknesses and deaths of the poor were rampant and this included mostly children. It was then that these Foundresses began to accept more orphans to their *Institute*, so that the number rose to more than a dozen girls" (Archives). This information indicates the extent of Mother Angela's openness and sensitivity to the needs of the time. It is this readiness to serve others that she transmitted to her spiritual daughters in the charism of the Congregation.

There are various forms of human misery. Certainly, the most poignant ones are those which befall persons through no fault of their own, for example, sickness. That is the reason why Mother Mary Angela attached such importance to having the sisters care for the sick.

In the *Spiritual Counsels* to Sister Mary Bogdana she cautioned: "Visit and help the sick, especially those who are most abandoned" (SW III, 134). She desired that this be a permanent service. In the *Directives Pertaining to the Congregation* she suggests that there be "at least four sisters always available who could be sent out to the sick in the city" (SW III, 172). The need for such services was always great because of a scarcity of those who were willing to perform them.

Mother was a realistic woman and she knew that the sisters would not find it possible to respond to all the needs. Overtaxing them with tasks might create serious difficulties in community life. However, the sisters' zealous undertakings of the various tasks resulted in the fact that the charism of the Congregation became clearer and more understood by those whom they served.

In another letter to the same sister, Mother truly rejoiced in the happiness of the sisters who were serving the sick. "[I can imagine] what joy it is for your hearts to know that in healing bodies you restore health to many a soul" (SW I, 114).

These and many other responses of Mary Angela testify to her authentic concern for the sick, always coupled with prudence and care for the good of the sisters. The ability to harmonize such essential elements of the life of the new Congregation called for great wisdom. To her can be attributed the praise in Scripture: "When one finds a worthy woman, her value is far beyond pearls" (Prv 31:10).

Conducting the Centers and aiding the sick are but a few ways in which Mary Angela actuated the commandment of love of neighbor. She herself, as well as her Congregation, fulfilled this commandment basically in two ways: the apostolate as evidence of the concern for the salvation of neighbors, and aid to the poor in their material poverty.

These forms of living the love of neighbor deserve individual study and they will be considered again in additional reflective readings.

PRAYER

Blessed Mary Angela, Foundress of the Congregation of the Felician Sisters
 – pray for us.
Guardian of children from the basements and attics of the poor
 – pray for us.
Persevering in concern for the salvation of souls
 – pray for us.

I do not ask you for an ideal love but for a love like yours which depends on sacrifice, on complete using up of oneself, on absolute forgetting of oneself, and on never seeking consideration for myself in anything or anywhere.

O Lord, you yourself recommend renunciation. I desire to renounce myself for others; I do not want to belong to myself but to sacrifice myself completely for others even though it would cost me a great deal (SW III, 73–74).

III

FULFILLMENT OF THE WILL OF GOD

*Let this fill you with joy in your present state;
let it suffice that you do the will of your Spouse,
that for his love you lead others to him, that in all
this you suffer and yearn, because you love or at
least with all your heart you desire to love Jesus*
(SW I, 109).

It is a great gift for a person to know the will of God.
Because of this, one is enabled to know how to conduct
oneself. By revealing his will God determines to enter
into a special relationship with the individual. This is a
relationship of intimacy and benevolence. However, in
revealing his will, God awaits the person's response of
acceptance of his will.

A similar situation exists in human interrelation-
ships, where a proper understanding and fulfillment
of another's will has a fundamental meaning in
strengthening the bonds of goodwill, friendship, and
love. This applies not only to individual relationships
in families and among friends, but also in work
places, in greater social group structures, and in civil
organizations. This also holds true for the heavenly
kingdom whose existence is most evidently the will of
God.

In the introduction to the Dogmatic Constitution of
the Church, *Lumen gentium*, Vatican Council II teaches
that "the eternal Father, in accordance with the utterly
gratuitous and mysterious design of his wisdom . . .
chose to raise up men to share in his own divine life
. . . and determined to call them together in a holy
Church" (LG I:2). "To carry out the will of the Father

Christ inaugurated the kingdom of heaven on earth and revealed to us his mystery; by his obedience he brought about our redemption" (LG I:3). "Exalted at God's right hand, he first received the promised Holy Spirit from the Father" (Acts 2:33). The Holy Spirit sanctifies the Church continuously, so that "consequently, those who believe might have access through Christ in one Spirit to the Father" (LG I:4). Thus is the history of salvation summarized as the realization of the eternal plan of God determined by an act of the free will of the one God in the Most Holy Trinity.

The comprehension of the plan of salvation is a revelation of the authority of God over the world. This means that God oversees the events in such a manner that the free actions of human beings are not capable of counteracting his eternal purposes. In teaching us how to pray the Lord Jesus tells us to say to the Father: "Thy will be done." In this way, he directs us to acknowledge that God wants only our good. Likewise, it is a sign of hope that our future is in the hands of God, but that we must submit to his will with a trusting heart.

The above cited Vatican Council II teaching pointed out that the most perfect example of obedience, joined with unbounded trust in the will God, is our Lord and Savior Jesus Christ, the Incarnate Son of the Eternal Father. Through his submission to the will of God, he revealed to us the kind of obedience expected of us. It is a total submission even to the sacrifice of life itself. In the Gospel according to St. John we read that the Lord Jesus received a command from the Father to lay down his life and then to take it up again (*cf.* Jn 10:18). This power of laying down and taking up his life again was proof to Jesus of the love of the Father (*cf.* Jn 10:17). Fulfilling the will of his Father was his food (*cf.* Jn 4:34). And for this reason, Jesus was obedient "accepting even death, death on the cross" (Phil 2:8).

Jesus gave us a unique lesson on obedience to the will of the Father in his prayer in the Garden of Olives.

The author of the Letter to the Hebrews wrote that "in the days when he was in the flesh, he offered prayers and supplications with loud cries and tears to God, who was able to save him from death" (Heb 5:7). According to the version of Mark the Evangelist, this was a truly piercing cry: "Abba (O Father), you have the power to do all things. Take this cup away from me. But let it be as you would have it, not as I" (Mk 14:36).

Christ's bone-chilling tone adds to his emotion-filled cry, "abba," a name used by Aramean children when addressing their fathers. The term could be freely translated as "daddy," but the official and accepted literal translation is "father." It expresses a strong emotional tie and portrays Christ's deep union with God the Father.

The Father, to whom Christ turns with such emotion at the time of his deepest distress and fears, is his own Father and, at the same time, Almighty God. Jesus pleaded: "Abba (O Father), you have the power to do all things" (Mk 14:36), which also signifies that he could avoid his cruel suffering on the cross. Does there really exist an earthly father whose heart would not shudder upon hearing such a fearful cry: "Daddy, Daddy." Apparently, his Heavenly Father was silent and remained silent to the last agony on the cross . . . To this cry is added the feeling of complete abandonment at the moment of death: "My God, my God, why have you forsaken me?" (Mk 15:34). What an inconceivable thing! Theologians justifiably confirm that the Paschal Mystery reveals not only the deep love of God for humankind, but also the unfathomable mystery of the Holy Trinity.

By his submission to the will of his Father, the Lord Jesus teaches us obedience to the will of God, irrespective to what it relates. Unfortunately most frequently, we accept the will of God with the expression, "Since it has to be this way, let it be." Jesus accepts the will of the Father well aware that "it doesn't have to be this way," because the Father can remove the chalice. He accepts it because it is the will of the Father whom he loves; in this way requiting the Father's love. Furthermore, perhaps what we find most difficult to accept in prayer during very trying times is the apparent lack of a visible "reaction" from God the Father, despite our sincere conviction of his omnipotent power and love for us. In our logic the inscrutability of God in his action towards us also escapes us. To this "lack" of a response our only "reaction" should be a closer walk in the footsteps Christ left in the Garden.

The perfection of fulfilling the Father's will by Jesus could give rise to the firm belief that no one is able even partly to imitate such a high ideal. For who can imitate God himself? In the meantime Jesus told those who wanted to come after him, to take up their crosses and follow in his footsteps (*cf.* Mk 8:34). The history of the Church demonstrates that there were great numbers of such heroic disciples who faithfully followed the Master, while at the same time leaving an example for others. St. Francis of Assisi is one such "fool" for God, who with every fiber of his body desired to imitate the Lord and Savior. Through his heroism he became an ideal for future generations of disciples. Among these also is Mother Mary Angela.

In his *Rule*, St. Francis encourages his friars to discern the will of God and to completely fulfill it. "We have left the world now"—the poor Mendicant of Assisi teaches—"and all we have to do is to be careful to obey God's will and please him" (Writings I, 47). Thus he points to the consequences of an undertaken decision and the value of fidelity to a given word. He considers fulfilling the divine will as his whole life-giving service to God. In his paraphrase of the *Lord's Prayer*, St. Francis understands "thy will be done" as "that we may love you with our whole heart [. . .] as best we can encouraging them all to love you" (Writings III, 160). The entire life of a friar ought to be focused upon drawing others to God in order to do good. Certainly, the good of an individual or of a community permits each person to discern the will of God. That is why the will of superiors, whose concern is the good of the community, is a sign of the will of God. Obedience to superiors is obedience to the will of God (*cf.* Writings I, 79). There will still be an occasion to get back to this topic.

St. Francis held a radical viewpoint concerning obedience to superiors. This radicalism is expressed in his *Admonitions* about perfect obedience: "A subject may realize that there are many courses of action that would be better and more profitable to his soul than that what his superior commands. In that case he should make an offering of his own will to God, and do his best to carry out what the superior enjoined" (Writings I, 79).

For contemporary individuals who value their own convictions, it might be beyond their comprehension to accept such a mode of behavior. But in the same *Admonitions*, St. Francis clarifies why it is necessary to relinquish one's convictions. In addition, he observes that such a subjective attitude is at most a pretext. Furthermore, it shows a lack of recognition of consequences, based on the fact that acceptance of the common life is a resignation of one's preferences and likes. Continued persistence in such an attitude is a return to the thinking of one's former way of life. For St. Francis it means looking back (*cf.* Lk 9:62), and going "back to their own will that they have given up" (Writings I, 80). This type of obedience is necessarily expected of the brothers. In his understanding, it was a sign of brotherly love in agreement with the counsel of St. Peter for whom genuine love of brothers, one for another, was expressed in obedience to each other (*cf.* 1 Pt 1:22).

For Mother Mary Angela, obedience was one of the most beautiful virtues. She desired to live it. However, she grieved that her obedience remained only a daydream, because she became a superior and was obliged to issue orders to others. In one of her *Meditations* she considered if she could ever even be obedient. "I sometimes wonder" she noted, "whether I would now be able to obey because when did I ever have the opportunity to learn how to do it?" (SW III, 69).

Actually, as the Foundress of the Congregation, even though she was not at the time a superior, she enjoyed a good measure of independence (*cf.* SW III, 69). At the same time she was fully aware that fulfilling the will of God could be learned through obedience to the will of her superiors. That is why she felt a great need and desire to practice obedience to someone. This explains her submission to Father Honorat Kozminski by her vow of uncompromising obedience to him (*cf.* SW II/1, 127–128; 137–138).

For beginners in the spiritual life it may seem strange that Mary Angela longed to become so dependent upon Father Honorat. Would she not feel sufficiently mature spiritually to be able to direct herself in her interior life? According to human logic this would seem most likely. Nevertheless, souls advanced in the way of perfection arrive at the conviction that they are incapable of objectively evaluating the state of their spiritual life. They feel the need of getting an objective opinion and obtaining verification. Otherwise, it is very easy to slip into a state of self-satisfaction or, even worse, into scrupulosity. Awareness of these missteps is also a mark of humility.

It is only natural that the Mother of the Felician Community deeply longed for spiritual direction with complete submission to Father Honorat. In one of her letters to him, she reminds him about his spiritual direction and her total obedience. "Whatever you decide, I will be entirely at peace because I desire nothing else but the fulfillment of God's will which I see in your will for me" (SW II/1, 56).

The obstacles in practicing obedience increased the desire of Mary Angela to unite her will most perfectly with the will of God, which she wished with all her heart to fulfill most precisely. In one of her written resolutions, she expressed the desire to carry the cross of Jesus in order to obtain the grace and strength to fulfill the will of God (*cf.* SW III, 86). In a letter to Father Honorat Kozminski (18 November 1866) regarding the love of obedience she wrote thus: "I especially love what seems to me to be the essence of religious life, namely, obedience" (SW II/1,194). Before she entered religious life, she mused about obedience. The desire for perfect obedience was linked with the feeling of its unattainability. These feelings arose not so much from a lack of understanding the full meaning of its essence, but rather from human weakness.

In her pursuit of perfection, Mother Angela drew much consolation from the experiences of St. Teresa of Avila. She recalls this in the *Spiritual Counsels* to Sister Mary Bogdana. She advises her to frequently pray thus to God: "Lord, teach me to do your will. Tell me what to do; I am ready for everything!" (SW III, 117). For her, this is the foundation of perfection. It is important always to fulfill the will of God and ever to unite one's will with his will, especially when difficulties arise and when it is time to take up some cross. Crosses come in various forms, sometimes very painful, especially when they come from people who insult or humiliate others. The patient bearing of these crosses leads to sanctity and fills the soul with enduring peace (*cf.* SW III, 117).

The faithful fulfillment of the will of God was not only Mother Angela's expression of love of God but also of love of neighbor. She understood it as an atonement to God for those who ignore his will and do not care to recognize it, do not accept it, and even rebel against it.

In a letter to Sister Mary Joseph she wrote: "Do not resist, my child, but allow God to do with you as he pleases. Trust him with all your heart. Let your submission to God's will atone for so many people who rebel against his holy will. At every moment of your life, even the most painful, repeat with Mary, 'Oh my God, let it be done to me according to your will'" (SW I, 156).

Blessed Mary Angela also understood the fulfillment of God's will as a means of unity with God. This is possible even in this life "when we desire and seek nothing but God's will, and when we cling to it with our whole heart" (SW I, 6). Such a radical surrender to his will is a guaranteed route to union in heaven.

The faithful fulfillment of God's will is possible, if a person discerns it well. Obviously, this does not relate to knowing his will as found in the commandments of God for these are generally known, but what about the case of God's will pertaining, for example, to a choice of vocation, or to arriving at some concrete decision even in minor matters. The Lord Jesus said, "If you can trust a person in little things, you can trust him in greater" (Lk 16:10). Any individual who loves God will certainly desire to know the will of God also in smaller matters.

The question of leaving Mary Angela in the cloister was an example of discerning the will of God in a concrete situation. While seeking an answer to this matter, she sought the counsel of Father Honorat. She believed that his advice would be a sign of the will of God for her (cf. SW II, 58). Frequently, his decisions helped her in discerning the will of God both in Congregational matters as well as in her own spiritual life.

It happened, too, that she would discern God's will through meditation upon the circumstances surrounding a given situation. Such was the case with the writing of the Constitutions of the Congregation (cf. SW II, 229). Obviously, Mother Angela was aware that the condition for discerning God's will is prayer, which is why she wrote in one of her letters to Father Honorat that "we must pray to see God's will in this matter" (SW II, 264). It is evident, then, that she tried to discern the will of God in three ways: through prayer, through meditation upon the surrounding circumstances, and through obedience to her superiors—in her case to Father Honorat, her spiritual director.

The discernment of God's will and its faithful fulfillment is crucial not only for members of communities and religious congregations. In ordinary life, situations often arise in which persons hope to make a choice agreeable with the will of God, because they sincerely desire good for themselves, their families, and friends. This could pertain, for example, to choosing a course of study, employment, marriage to a certain person, or the like. The stance of Mother Angela, as expressed in her counsels and experiences, can help in discerning the will of God.

The first indispensable step which should be taken in order to know God's will is prayer. Prayer helps a person to be open to the signs of God's Providence and also to the acceptance of his will.

Next, one must analyze the possible indicators through which God reveals his will and reflect how this action relates to one's existing responsibilities.

Finally, it is recommended to bring the decision to one's confessor or spiritual director, should there be one, or eventually to persons well qualified in the area related to the decision.

The persevering and humble search for the will of God surely will not go without an answer. After all, God told us that his command is not up in the sky, nor across the sea. If such is the case, we cannot excuse ourselves and claim ignorance. God's word is very near us, it is in our hearts and we have only to carry it out (cf. Dt 30:11–14).

PRAYER

Blessed Mary Angela, Foundress of the Congregation of the Felician Sisters
– pray for us.
Admirable example of Franciscan goodness and compassion
– pray for us.
Blessed Mary Angela, who in suffering praised and loved the will of God
– pray for us.

Teach me to suffer with such silence, such purity and such love as your most pure Mother suffered when you left her as an orphan on this earth. Allow me, O Jesus, as you allowed her to die from pain, from longing, and from love, and then do with me whatever you please.

Allow me to love you forever, to suffer for you forever, if it be your will. I only want to live in your love, to be yours forever, and to praise your divine will forever (SW III, 14–15).

IV

PRAYER

Try to heed the call of Jesus to pray always and never to cease. The Lord gave you the spirit of prayer, so try to maintain it during the day amidst your duties and try to practice constant interior prayer in union with Our Lord. Remember that not only does this gift of God oblige you to such an effort, but also your religious vocation demands it (Letter to Sister Mary Joseph, SW I, 154).

Prayer is an expression of faith, hope, and love. Prayer also strengthens these. There is a direct interdependence of prayer and these virtues which we call theological. If we stop to reflect honestly on our faith, we must first examine what our daily prayer is like. Prayer reflects our yearning for God, it strengthens the hope of receiving what he has promised, and it is our answer to the love of God for us.

The example of Jesus Christ witnesses to the importance of prayer in a person's life. He, the incarnate Son of God the Father, prays always. In order to pray, he often goes to the Mountain (*cf.* Mt 14:23), and prays in seclusion (*cf.* Lk 9:18), even when he is being sought (*cf.* Mk 1:37). He prays not only because he wishes to remain alone in silence with his beloved Father but because his prayer is totally linked with his mission.

We know this in virtue of the reference to the prayer of Jesus before such important occurrences as: the baptism in the Jordan (*cf.* Lk 3:21), the calling of the Twelve (*cf.* Lk 6:12), the transfiguration on Mount Tabor (*cf.* Lk 9:29), and the entrusting of the prayer

Our Father to the apostles (*cf.* Lk 11:1). The link of the prayer of Jesus with his mission is most obviously seen during the forty days of his stay in the desert (*cf.* Mt 4:7).

From this it follows that we have before us a very important lesson: every apostolic endeavor is to be preceded with fervent prayer. Mother Mary Angela adhered to this lesson always, especially then when she had to make any decisions regarding the Congregation (*cf.* SW II/1, 163).

A form of prayer frequently used by Jesus was the prayer of petition. It is an intercessory prayer, flowing directly from his redemptive mission (*cf.* Heb 7:25) and from his function as the Mediator between humankind and God (*cf.* 1 Tim 2:5; Heb 9:15). Besides the prayer of intercession, Jesus prayed the prayer of praise in which he expresses his joy in being able to manifest the deeds of the Lord. An example of this is his hymn of praise, "I offer you praise, O Father, Lord of heaven and earth, because what you have hidden from the learned and the clever you have revealed to the merest children" (Lk 10:21). Here the Evangelist notes that this praise was expressive of joy in the Holy Spirit (*cf.* Lk 10:21a). This was an important observation, for it indicates the involvement of the Holy Spirit in the prayer of the Lord Jesus who praises the Father in the Holy Spirit.

This fact has a fundamental meaning for our prayer, because it points out that our prayer also should be "in the Holy Spirit." St. Paul in his letter to the Galatians teaches this clearly: "The proof that you are sons is the fact that God has sent forth into our hearts the spirit of his Son, which cries 'Abba!' ('Father!')" (Gal 4:6). Since we have the same Spirit as did Jesus, we also are able, as he did, to turn to our Father who is in Heaven and cry "Abba!"

The most sublime and at the same time the most difficult prayer is the prayer of the Lord Jesus in the

Garden of Olives (*cf.* Mk 14:36). It was already considered in connection with abiding by God's will. It is an intercession full of trust and ardent love for the Father, and also for the people who will attain salvation because of the Lord Jesus' obedience to the will of his Father. His prayer on the cross (*cf.* Mk 15:34) is likewise an expression of his everlasting union with the Father. Thus then, in a very practical way, the Lord Jesus indicates that we ought to pray without ceasing. He speaks of this clearly in the parable about the persistent widow and the importunate friend (*cf.* Lk 18:1–5; 11:5–8). That is also why St. Paul constantly reminds us that our prayer should be "unceasing" (*cf.* 2 Thes 1:3) and "at every opportunity" (Eph 6:18). It is this kind of teaching about prayer that Blessed Mary Angela desired to incorporate into her life, often giving up even sleep just so that she could pray (*cf.* SW III, 161).

Prayer is an extremely important element in the spiritual life of every Christian. The *Catechism of the Catholic Church* clarifies the fact that the revelation of the mystery of the Father through Jesus Christ in the Holy Spirit requires that the faithful live this mystery in a personal relationship with the Three-in-One God. "This personal relationship is prayer" (CCC 2558). This is a very broad definition of prayer. The *Catechism* cites one of the more concrete varieties of prayer characteristic of persons living in close union with God. St. Thérèse of the Child Jesus understood it thus: "For me, prayer is a surge of the heart; it is a simple look turned toward heaven; it is a cry of recognition; and of love embracing both trial and joy" (CCC 2558).

Much can be said about prayer. It is, after all, a topic most suitable for reflection. In this brief presentation it is impossible to bring to mind even the most essential truths about prayer. Fortunately, however, there is a synopsis of the teachings of the Church on this topic with which everyone can and ought to become fully acquainted. It is in the *Catechism* in Part Four which is devoted to Christian prayer (CCC 2558–2865).

It is worth while, however, to draw attention at least to the one aspect of prayer which St. Francis of Assisi strongly underscored. In his *Admonitions* on poverty he notes that there are such persons who spend all their time at prayer and other religious exercises, and mortify themselves by long fasts. But let an unpleasant word be directed at them and they fly into a rage. Such an attitude is a denial of the evangelical hatred of oneself (*cf.* Lk 14:26), which is a requisite of the perfect following of Jesus (*cf.* Writings I, 83).

Mother Mary Angela realized fully that prayer must go hand in hand with love of neighbor. After all, Jesus very directly said: "None of those who cry out, 'Lord, Lord,' will enter the kingdom of God but only the one who does the will of my Father in heaven" (Mt 7:21). Mindful of these words she used to remind the sisters how important is the union of prayer with good deeds. Effective prayer is dependent on good deeds and is related to the heroicity of virtues, especially obedience, denial of self, and self-giving.

It is to this method of practicing prayer that Mother encouraged Sister Mary Hedwig as well as many others (*cf.* SW I, 117). At the same time she begged Sister Mary Joseph to remain steadfastly in prayer, uniting it with her daily duties because—thanks to this combination she would retain a constant union with Jesus Christ. Prayer is God's gift (*cf.* SW I, 154). This form of prayer is particularly adaptable for lay persons living in such situations wherein daily responsibilities do not allow much time for prayer.

It is difficult to imagine that persons consecrated to the exclusive service of God would not remain in continual contact with him. To constantly remain in such oneness is the very essence of religious life. The means for such contact is precisely prayer, described very often as conversation with God. Now, conversation obviously entails not only speaking but also listening. We pray not only for the purpose of begging God for something or thanking him, but also for the purpose of recognizing his will and uniting ourselves more closely with him, just as friends and spouses do who live with each other and discuss everything together. Mother Mary Angela was totally aware of the value of prayer. She considered it a treasure. She instilled this conviction in her spiritual daughters. In her *Spiritual Counsels* to Sister Mary Bogdana she wrote: "Prayer is our full treasure. Whoever prays receives everything. That day, in which we omit meditation, is a lost day" (SW III, 118).

Just as conversation with those closest to us can be carried on in various circumstances, for instance, at table, at work, and even in the street, so likewise our prayer, understood as conversing with the Lord Jesus and abiding with him, can take on varieties of possibilities.

The Foundress of the Felician Sisters used many various prayer forms, and numerous pious practices. Most often they were: meditation, adoration of the Blessed Sacrament, the rosary, the Divine Office, the Way of the Cross, meditation on the Passion of Christ, examens, retreats, monthly days of reparation, and spiritual reading (*cf.* SW III, 235–236).

Obviously, these prayers were also adopted by the sisters. The above listed prayer forms and pious practices can be used by today's laity. It stands to reason that is important first to become acquainted with them and practice them somewhat regularly in order to benefit from their salutary power. The *Catechism of the Catholic Church* mentions three basic forms of prayer: vocal prayer, meditation, and contemplative prayer (*cf.* CCC 2700–2724). The simplest and most popular prayer form is, of course, vocal prayer such as the rosary and other devotional prayers.

For many people, unfortunately, these two types of prayer can become "mechanical rattling," so that, for them, it somehow is not perceived as conversation with Jesus. Still, this difficulty cannot be a reason to give up on these recitations. These can be strengthened, for example, through reading of the New Testament and meditation on the essence of the meaning of the words of the prayer or the particular mysteries of the faith of the rosary; or, if possible, praying before the tabernacle in adoration of the Lord Jesus present there under the appearance of bread.

Mother Mary Angela watched carefully that her spiritual daughters never neglected their prayer life. Since she believed that, if in accord with the *Constitutions* of the Congregation, the sisters devote themselves to apostolic activity, they are also obliged to be faithful to their prayer life. Neglect in this matter leads to impoverishment of the interior life, resulting in the sisters being swept into a vortex of activities with the loss of their interior stability (*cf.* SW II/2, 250).

Those who had already allowed themselves to fall into this turmoil realize how great the danger thereof is. These individuals accuse themselves of forgetting about morning prayers, and in the evening they barely manage to make the *sign of the cross* and pray a *Glory be to the Father*. This positively is insufficient to give any credence to the actual reason for one's activities, even though by its nature it is directed towards the good of the neighbor.

When prayer life proceeds properly, each encounter with the Loving and the Beloved One becomes a source of joy. However, joyous moments during prayer are not yet indicators of its perfection. They are gifts of God given so that the beginners on the road of prayer can be encouraged to work on self-improvement and on perfecting the bond with him who is all Love.

It is important to remember that praying cannot be regarded as a source of pleasure. Such prayer becomes an indication of egoism and the search for self-satisfaction rather than a yearning for God's glory and for the purification of one's soul. Spiritual directors very frequently call attention to this.

Blessed Mary Angela also was aware of this danger and, in a letter to Sister Mary Aniela, she imparted very valued advice on the matter. She reminded her that in her prayer she should not seek her own gratification but only God's glory. The difficulties in prayer are evidence of the fact that a person needs purification, and so she reminded her: "The more our prayer seems tiresome, dry, difficult, and fraught with temptation, so much the better it is [. . .]. Humble yourself before God and bear your trial patiently" (SW I, 32).

Distractions and inner feelings of dryness are not the only difficulties in prayer. Serious doubts as to whether there is any reason for praying can be created by an apparent lack of response to petitions. Mary Angela gave Father Honorat her explanation of this kind of difficulty in one of her letters. In it she complains that prayers addressed to God for the Congregation do not bring anticipated results. She firmly believed that this is so because their petitions are not supported by acts of penance which resemble those practiced by St. Francis of Assisi and his brothers.

In Mother Angela's opinion the penitential practices of the Congregation are not severe enough since radical poverty is not practiced. It is not extreme poverty because "we do not suffer the least want; all our needs are satisfied" (SW II/1,108). This conviction can well be attributed to her desire to personally empty herself of everything for the Lord Jesus. From other sources, however, it is known that the circumstances of life and work under which the sisters lived were far from luxurious.

Granted that seeking joy in prayer may be an indication of imperfection, it does not preclude the possibility of desiring consolation in prayer in times of suffering or sorrow. Prayer at such times becomes a petition for help which God never refuses to his children. St. James the Apostle, in fact, very directly encourages it. "If any one of you is suffering hardship, that one must pray" (Jas 5:13). With this advice Mary Angela encouraged Sister Mary Hedwig and Sister Mary Joseph to perseverance in prayer in their anxieties and temptations, so that this prayer would preserve them from excessive dwelling on their wounded souls and difficult experiences (*cf.* SW I, 101; 152).

Prayer leads to a more perfect union with God. In a letter to Sister Mary Aniela, Mother Angela clarifies that the pinnacle of perfection is precisely this union and that it is twofold: "first, the union of our whole being with God; the other, the union of our will with the will of God. This first union we will attain in heaven, the second union we ought to begin striving for in this life; and it is accomplished then when we desire and seek nothing but God's will, and when we cling to it with our whole heart" (SW I, 26).

In the discussion on living the will of God we already spoke about how to seek the will of God and how to discern it. In Mary Angela's interior life, it was precisely prayer that helped her to discern the will of God. In prayer she sought enlightenment from God, especially in matters related to the Congregation (*cf.* SW II/1, 163; 35–36). Her example of humble and fervent prayer is worthy of imitation also in our times, and not only by her spiritual daughters but also by all who desire a closer union with the Triune God.

PRAYER

Blessed Mary Angela, Foundress of the Congregation of the Felician Sisters
- pray for us.
A love of prayer
- obtain for us, Mary Angela.
A spirit of service and love for the Church
- obtain for us, Mary Angela

Give me, your servant, a sincere and genuine fervor which would help me to uphold your glory.

Give me the strength and courage of which I need such a great deal, in order to inflame the indifferent, awaken the slothful, chastise the erring, and increase the fervor of your devoted and dear spouses (SW III, 19).

V

THE APOSTOLATE

Give aid to all without exception; your vocation obliges you not to exclude anyone, for everybody is our neighbor. I know I need not encourage you to self-giving for you will not neglect anything, nor will you think of yourself, but only the glory God, of the common good, and that your aim will be the salvation of souls which will be your greatest concern, and that you will not get involved in other matters, being mindful of your calling and your position (Letter to Sister Mary Hedwig, SW I, 112).

The apostolate is one of the important topics in the writings of the Foundress of the Felician Sisters. Although Mother Mary Angela usually referred to apostolic service as the work for the salvation of souls or the endeavor towards it, yet it remains nothing else but precisely that—the apostolate. As a reminder of the teaching of the Vatican Council II, the *Catechism of the Catholic Church* affirms that that we call an apostolate "every activity of the Mystical Body that aims to spread the Kingdom of Christ over all the earth" (CCC 863). In the light of this definition the entire work of Mother could be recognized as apostolic ministry.

Her striving for the good of souls and for their salvation flowed from an ardent love of God and neighbor, while its concrete forms were the fruit of her reflective prayer. Her entire apostolic ministry flowed from prayer and was suffused with prayer. When she could no longer participate actively in the apostolate, she supported her spiritual daughters with prayer and penance.

Her attitude harmonizes perfectly with the actual teaching of the Church on apostolic ministry and prayer. "In keeping with their vocations, the demands of the times, and the various gifts of the Holy Spirit,"—states the *Catechism*—"the apostolate assumes the most varied forms. But charity, drawn from the Eucharist above all, is always the soul of the whole apostolate" (CCC 864).

The apostolic service of Mary Angela correlates with the ministry of the bishops, the successors of the Apostles. To them particularly the Lord Jesus entrusted the care for the spread of the Gospel, when before his departure from this earth, he said: "Go, therefore, and make disciples of all the nations. Baptize them in the name of the Father and of the Son and of the Holy Spirit" (Mt 28:19). Even before that during his public ministry, he sent seventy-two of his disciples to every town and place he intended to visit (*cf.* Lk 10:1). Just as these seventy-two disciples prepared the people for a meeting with Jesus, so do the laity with their apostolic activity ready the soil for the ministry of the bishops and the priests. Each member of the Church —by virtue of Baptism—is called to proclaim the Gospel by one's whole life, because of its very nature the Church is apostolic. The Vatican Council II *Decree on the Apostolate of Lay People* states: "The laity are made to share in the priestly, prophetical, and kingly office of Christ; they have therefore, in the Church and in the world, their own assignment in the mission of the whole People of God" (AA 2). Long before the clear formulation of this teaching, many lay persons were actively involved in this threefold function of Christ, for example, in founding of religious orders and communities as did St. Francis of Assisi. Obviously, the Foundress of the Felician Sisters belongs in this company.

For Mother Mary Angela, St. Francis was a splendid model of one working for the salvation of others. She was convinced that had he not been engaged wholeheartedly in this work, perhaps he "might not have received the stigmata" (SW I, 89). Actually he devoted himself entirely to the salvation of others, not excluding magistrates, consuls, judges, and governors from all over the world. In the *Letter to the Rulers of Nations* he reminded them not to forget "God or swerve from his commandments" (Writings II, 116). Furthermore, in his *Rule* St. Francis advised his friars to go to all people and exhort them to praise God (*cf.* Writings I, 46). An analogous command is enclosed in the *Letter to a General Chapter* (*cf.* Writings II, 104). Similar apostolic zeal burned in the heart of Mother Mary Angela.

Her sphere of activity in the apostolate, and likewise of her spiritual daughters, was widespread. The sisters operated Centers (a forerunner of parish schools) and were concerned with bringing up children. They taught catechism and prepared catechumens, organized Sunday reading sessions, tended to the sick and wounded, lead rosary groups, conducted retreats, directed Secular Franciscan groups, visited the sick and the lonely homebound and provided them with spiritual direction, and attended to the care of churches. Above all, the goal of their apostolic ministry was primarily the following: to teach the people about Christ and bring him to them; to inform them of his love and concern for the salvation of their own souls and those of others; to foster devotion to the Mother of God; and to give a personal witness of living a moral life.

This abundance of apostolic initiatives demanded complete dedication of the sisters as well as an effective organization of their time. Mother watched carefully that this external activity would not inhibit their interior life. In the *Observations on the Constitutions* she noted that "superiors should watch that the spirit of dedication should not kill the spiritual life, but rather that the latter always should be the basis of the former" (SW III, 211). Experience, however, proves how difficult it is to maintain that proper balance!

Fulfillment of apostolic tasks always demands proper preparation. Mother Mary Angela was well aware of this. She encouraged the sisters to strive to the best of their ability to continue to acquaint themselves with all the aspects of their apostolate "and to learn all the jobs of the peasants so that at all times and in all works they could be a good example. This, above all else, will help to bring them close to the sisters. In this way the sisters will gain their confidence" (SW III, 156).

Mother paid particular attention to a solid preparation for the work with children in the Centers (SW II/2, 125) and later in the schools. In order to prepare for required examinations and to prepare to teach according to an accepted system, some of the sisters studied under the tutelage of professors (SW II/1, 41). She also reminded the sisters that they should study the catechism conscientiously and strive to acquire a general knowledge of world affairs which is necessary for the apostolate (*cf.* SW II/2, 42; III, 170).

The sisters' underlying field of apostolic activity was to bring spiritual assistance to persons who were enduring various experiences of suffering. Mother rejoiced at the news from Sister Mary Hedwig that, in some cases while helping the poor in temporal needs, they were able to "restore health to many a soul" (SW I, 114; 129). At another time Mother zealously encouraged her to patiently await the realization of her own desires and continue to persevere in her dedication to the good of the peasants among whom she was chosen to work. Mary Angela pleaded strongly: "do not desert them, do not be deterred by any hardships from saving their souls" (SW I, 138).

In taking care of the sick the sisters also conformed to this goal. Mother wanted the sisters to be very concerned with the health of their charges and to have basic knowledge of illnesses in order to better serve the patients. She was justifiably convinced that "in rendering care for the body of the sick, a sister could more easily influence the soul" (SW II/1, 155). On this subject of visiting the sick, she wrote to Father Honorat that excusing themselves from this would not be in accord with the vocation of the sisters. "This seems to me contrary to our vocation which obliges us to a dedication without limits. It certainly does not behoove the sisters to excuse themselves whenever they are called, unless there is a real impossibility. All the more, that in ministering to the sick, the sisters can bring help not only for the body but they can also influence the soul" (SW II, 240).

She also recommended that the sisters visit the sick in their homes. She suggested "that there should be at least four sisters always available who could be sent out to the sick in the city" (SW III, 172). On the other hand, depending on available vacancies, older and incapacitated persons should be admitted to the institution. The sisters in charge were to tend to all their needs and, above all, to provide proper spiritual exercises for them; they were to encourage them, keep up their spirits, and prepare them for a happy death (*cf.* SW III, 166).

A very important aspect of the apostolate of Mother Mary Angela and the sisters of her Congregation was the care of children, especially the poor. It was precisely this gathering of the children and their care that became the nucleus of the Felician apostolate. From her early years Sophia always had a great empathy for poor children whose fathers were addicted to alcohol and wasted away the family income. She knew of these cases from her father who was the prosecutor for the probate court in Kalisz. Later she was able to witness this misery firsthand in Warszawa. And so, she decided to organize a shelter for poor children and homeless elderly women. She leased two small attic rooms on Koscielna 10 Street in Warszawa and there she gathered the children from the cellars and attics of impoverished families, together with poverty-stricken elderly women. At first, her parents provided the funds for this initiative, but later she sought assistance from additional donors.

Mother Mary Angela very carefully planned the administration and organization of a future project which she called the *Institute*. In her first letter to Father Honorat, she presented her plan to him and even included the daily schedule for the children and the women. She determined to have the children taught reading, writing as well as arithmetic, and did not neglect to include playtime. As regards their religious education she planned to concentrate on bible history and catechism. However, the study of catechism would be preceded by learning the prayers combined with the explanation of the *Lord's Prayer*, the *Hail Mary* and the *I Believe in God*.

She was concerned that the lessons not be solely theoretical, but be supported by practical examples. The children's study of prayers also included instruction on the method for the examination of conscience (*cf.* SW II/1, 15; 28). For the children, her primary concern was the moral issue. She was aware that to attempt to teach them pious practices was not an easy task because they tend to be constantly distracted. She wanted "these children to be genuinely pious, to prompt them to piety, and not to discourage or fatigue them" (SW II/1, 29). She also was solicitous about preparing them properly for confession and for being attentive to a confessor's lesson and to sermons.

Mother grieved over the plight of the poor children of Warszawa and even more over their demoralization. She felt a great need to expand all efforts in their upbringing, especially in the case of the difficult children. She was so convinced of this that she wrote to Father Honorat in one of her letters: "I was told that if they are unruly, they must be dismissed so that they would not corrupt others and that the *Institute* is not a reformatory but an educational institution. Though this is the opinion of the superiors, I disagree. It seems to me, that the worse a child is, the more it is necessary to work with her in order to help her overcome those evil tendencies. We should not dismiss children or else we could lose them completely" (SW II/1, 29).

The situation with the elderly women whom Mother Angela hoped to influence morally was quite a different matter. Her care for them was motivated by the hope that they could dedicate the remainder of their lives to God. But this proved to be a difficult task because the women were accustomed to freedom and were not willing to submit to the rigor of the *Institute* which they considered to be just a shelter. Their attitude impeded any kind of spiritual help. Mother agreed to remove the majority of them, which then provided additional room for children, especially for the sick ones (*cf.* SW II/1, 21).

Poverty was rampant during the lifetime of Mary Angela. Because of this, local parish communities could not responsibly upkeep their churches. The sisters, witnessing these difficulties, intended to help them. For example, Mary Angela determined to sew an altar cloth for a chapel in Lwow (*cf.* SW I, 64). She told Sister Mary Aniela to "spend Saturdays working for the poor churches" (SW I, 33). She praised Sister Mary Hedwig for her care of a neglected church, suggesting also that she try to involve other persons who would be able to help materially because the Congregation was not in a position to cover any costs involved (*cf.* SW I, 82). She permitted the sisters to decorate the altars in churches but without assuming "responsibility for any expenses" (SW I, 86). This was understandable because funds were barely sufficient for the upkeep of the sisters.

All the observations and counsels of Mother Mary Angela on the subject of the apostolate for her spiritual daughters are summarized in her directives on the topic of apostolic service through ordinary daily living in an extraordinary way. She wrote these even before there were *Constitutions* for the Congregation because the sisters assuming work in the Centers, which were far from the motherhouse community, needed guidance on how to live in order to bring glory to God and the good of their neighbor.

In the introduction to her *Short Directives* from around 1860, she reminded the sisters about the essence of their vocation. It consists in striving to save oneself and to save others by witnessing to them a life of Christian perfection. Because of this, people seeing the goodness in your acts will give praise to the heavenly Father (*cf.* Mt 5:16).

And this is how she understood such a life: "This perfection should not depend on extraordinary things, but on a common life lived in an uncommon way. Whatever they will do, let them do perfectly so that it may be said of them what was said of Christ: 'He has done everything well'" (SW III, 152). "An ordinary life lived in an extraordinary way"—that is the Felician ideal. This ideal is difficult to realize—as anyone who tried to live even a single ordinary day in an extraordinary way very well knows. It was thus that Mother Mary Angela spent her whole life!

O Jesus, give me at least one such day!

This exceptional lesson of Mother can be of benefit to everyone, not only to her spiritual daughters. Regardless of life's circumstances every Christian is called to perfection. The words of Our Lord Jesus in the sermon on the Mount, to which Mary Angela referred (Mt 5:16), are directed to all disciples, not only to religious sisters and religious brothers. Obviously, religious communities have at their disposal certain means which facilitate this pursuit of perfection, but every person in the world who desires this life will most certainly be given the necessary grace to pursue it. The example of Blessed Aniela Salawa bears witness to this. The first step is simply to desire it!

PRAYER

Blessed Mary Angela, Foundress of the Congregation of
the Felician Sisters
    – pray for us.
Wise educator of youth
    – pray for us.
Apostle of truth and evangelical love
    – pray for us.

*Tell me, O Lord, what should I do? On what road
will I meet you and see you? I will go there and I will
do everything you will demand of me* (SW III, 58).

VI

THE FACE OF CHRIST

Our Lord accepted the cross out of obedience to his Father's will. He took up the cross voluntarily, not out of compulsion but out of love. He yearned for the cross because he came on this earth to suffer. He did not abandon the cross even when he fell beneath its weight. He blessed those who crucified him. Suspended on the cross and satiated with pain, he did not complain that he had enough but desired to suffer more. He did not descend from the cross when they taunted him to do so—even though it would have been easy to do it (SW I, 42).

The wisdom of Sirach reminds us of the close connection between the heart of a person and his countenance (*cf.* Sir 13:24). The face is a mirror of the person's heart and that is why the encounter of two persons face to face with each other leads to a deeper mutual understanding of each other. The human longing for knowledge of God is symbolized in one's longing for the face of God. Although in no way is it like unto a human face, God, as one full of goodness (*cf.* Ps 4:7) or anger (*cf.* Is 54:8), can still reveal it to human beings. It is true that the Lord "used to speak to Moses face to face, as one man speaks to another" (Ex 33:11); yet when Moses requested to see the face of God, God said to him: you shall see my back; but my face is not to be seen (*cf.* Ex 33:23). St. Gregory of Nyssa commented on this fact by bringing to our attention that here we are dealing with a call to follow God. St. Gregory is convinced that following somebody means observing him from behind. That is how Moses—in his desire to see God—learned that he can do it only by imitating him and going wherever he goes. Thus, in our earthly life we also can see the face of God by following him faithfully, which means by doing his will. Such contemplation of the face of Christ ought to lead, and does lead, many to a faithful imitation of him.

Our Lord Jesus called his disciples to follow him as he imparted his last instruction to them during his farewell speech. He said to them: "You know the way that leads where I go" (Jn 14:4). When it became evident that the disciples did not understand everything completely and began to question him about the Father, then Jesus answered them: "Whoever has seen me has seen the Father" (Jn 14:9).

This method of knowing and imitating Christ leads also to knowing the Father. This is a conclusion of extreme significance, since in knowing Christ as the Son of God, we also learn to know the Father, and consequently we know the Holy Trinity. At the same time however, we must take note of the fact that Jesus spoke of knowing his Father just before his Passion. This, therefore, means that in knowing the scourged, crowned with thorns, and crucified Christ, we also know the Father. "It is the Father"—Jesus says—"who lives in me accomplishing his works" (Jn 14:10). The Father also lives in his Son during his Passion. In the bloodied, spat upon, and bruised disfigured face of the Lord is hidden also the face of the Father. What a tremendous sorrow this must be, a sorrow doubly deplorable because it is provoked by contempt of the beloved Son, and secondly by rejection of this very great love of the Father who loved the world so much that he gave his only Son (*cf.* Jn 3:16).

In contemplating the sufferings of Christ and led by the Holy Spirit, Mother Mary Angela constantly gazed upon the Crucified Lord. From him she learned about doing God's will. With her whole heart she longed to imitate him. In her meditations on the Passion of Christ she gathered enough strength to carry her own cross and to strengthen her spiritual daughters. For instance, in answer to the complaints of Sister Mary Hedwig who bemoaned the difficulties in accepting suffering, Mother wrote: "Christ himself wanted to console and teach us by example, so that although we see in ourselves an abhorrence of suffering we do not lose heart. He, the Omnipotent, sacrificed himself to death out of love. He trembled, feared, and even asked that the chalice be removed from him when the time came for him to drink of it; yet he consummated his holocaust" (SW I, 89). Perseverance in bearing the suffering is a mark of love for the Divine Spouse. In the remaining part of this letter Mother returns to this truth again.

In her *Act of Offering* of herself to the Lord Jesus, Mother Angela begged God for the ability to suffer without looking for any kind of consolation. She fervently prayed: "Teach me to suffer without seeking any consolation; to suffer without craving the sympathy of creatures; to suffer without even expecting the eternal joys of heaven. Teach me to suffer, not because suffering is the source of merit and glory, but because it unites us to you and makes our hearts like unto your Sacred Heart" (SW III, 14).

This prayer expresses how great and how unselfish Mother's love was. Aflame with such love, she likewise reminds us of the real meaning of any suffering which is offered to Christ. She cautioned Sister Mary Hedwig that once we dedicate ourselves to the Lord, we no longer belong to ourselves nor do we have any reason to be concerned about ourselves: "Look upon Christ as a sacrifice and try to emulate him. From him you will gather strength and courage" (SW I, 81).

In the last years of her life, this gazing upon the suffering Christ—Christ as a Sacrifice—evolved for her into the veneration of the Face of Christ. This cult of the Face of Christ developed and expanded in the Church many years before and was connected to the veil of St. Veronica which, as a relic, was frequently exposed for veneration in Rome.

In Poland this veneration of the Face of Christ was practiced already in the beginning of the thirteenth century, through the efforts of the Canoness Sisters of the Holy Spirit of Krakow. After a miracle which occurred during one of the expositions of the veil of St. Veronica in Rome in 1849, this cult of the Face of Christ began to spread rapidly especially in France. An Archcommission of the Holy Face was organized in Tours, France in 1884–1885. The Felician Sisters came in contact with it in Belgium in the same years, and Sister Mary Simplicia took it upon herself to popularize it in the Congregation. With the consent of the bishop of Krakow, it was established in the Krakow Diocese in 1894 and the Felician Sisters became the promoters of the cult.

Mother Angela very frequently prayed prostrated before the picture of the Holy Face of Christ. At the present time, this picture remains at the side altar of the Blessed Virgin Mary in the Felician Sisters Church in Krakow. It brings to our minds not only the Passion of the Lord and our call to imitate him, but also her who frequently renewed the sacrifice of her life before this image.

Today the cult of the Holy Face is less popular in the Church. It is ours to renew the fervor of this practice, not only because of the example of Mother Angela but also because of the instruction of Pope John Paul II in his Apostolic Letter *Novo millennio ineunte*. As he commented on the words of the Gospel: "We wish to see Jesus" (Jn 12:21), the Holy Father reminded us that the Church has an obligation to "reflect the light of Christ in every historical period" (NMI, 16a). As members of his Church we will not fulfill this obligation, unless we ourselves first determine to contemplate the face of Christ. John Paul II urges us to continual contemplation.

The fruit of the Great Jubilee Year of 2000 was precisely to have been the keener contemplation of the face of Christ (*cf.* NMI, 16b). John Paul II offers us some thoughts on such contemplation of the suffering face of Christ. He turns our attention to two occurrences during the Passion of Christ: as a son of God, his call to "Abba" and the cry from the cross. Both of these witness to the fact that "his passion is more than an experience of physical pain; his passion is an agonizing suffering of the soul" (NMI, 26). John Paul II reminds us that this is "the mystery within a mystery, before which we cannot but prostrate ourselves in adoration" (NMI, 25a).

When we gaze upon this holy Face of Jesus covered with bloody perspiration, treacherously kissed, and struck in the face amid blasphemies, we grasp more fully this unspeakably great mystery of our salvation. We must also realize our responsibility for the face of others, in accord with the words of Christ: "I assure you, as often as you did it for one of my least brothers, you did it for me" (Mt 25:40).

Would that there never be tears on the face of my neighbor! Would that there never be pain caused by my negligence or deception!

In this mystery, the possibility of seeing the face of Christ by imitating him opens up for us a new dimension. With that mystery is linked the mystery of the Church. Today, those who wish to see Christ and in him the Father cannot search anywhere but in Christ's Church. The face of Christ is reflected in the face of the Church. This is the action of the Holy Spirit.

And so it is that the Church, energized by the Holy Spirit is the center in which each person experiences the love of God the Father. Just as Philip gazing with faith on his Teacher was able to recognize the Father (*cf.* Jn 14:9–11), thus also every individual looking at the mystical body of Christ which is the Church, is able to recognize the benign presence of the Father who causes that "the sun rises on the bad and the good" (Mt 5:45). As members of the Church, each of us individually, should feel obligated to reflect some characteristic features of the Face of Christ that others can recognize in us. They will perceive these only when we, in imitation of Christ, faithfully do his will.

PRAYER

Blessed Mary Angela, Foundress of the Congregation of the Felician Sisters
 – pray for us.
Gifted by the Creator with sensitivity to pain and human misery
 – pray for us.
Given to penance for the sins of neighbor and the world
 – pray for us.

O Lord Jesus Christ, presenting ourselves before your adorable face to ask for the graces we most need, we beseech above all that you might grant us the gift of never refusing at any time to do what you request of us through your commandments and divine inspirations.

O good Jesus, who has said "Ask and you shall receive, seek and you shall find, knock and it shall be opened to you," give us the faith which obtains all, and supply the trust which we lack; grant us in your love, and for your eternal glory, the graces which we need and which we look for from your infinite mercy.

Adorable Face of Jesus, my love, my light, my life, grant that I may serve, know, and love you alone, and that I may live with you and for you.

Eternal Father, I offer you the adorable Face of your beloved Son, for the honor and glory of your Name, the conversion of sinners and the salvation of the dying (Prayer to the Holy Face, FBP, 44–45).

VII

PERSEVERANCE
IN SUFFERING AND SOLITUDE

Your sacrifice of yourself is very pleasing to him; try to persevere in that spirit of sacrifice, and do not be overcome by adversity. Do not be discouraged; rather let all difficulties be an impetus to ever greater zeal and fidelity to God's service. Rejoice even when Jesus gives you the opportunity to show him how much you love him, because true love manifests itself not in emotions but in suffering and in bearing much for the love of God. No wonder that Jesus sends you such an abundance of vexations because you should be a rock on which future generations can rest; and the more the billows strike against this rock, the more durable and immovable it becomes (SW I, 71–72).

A persevering person is one who strives to attain a chosen goal, regardless of the difficulties and obstacles on the way—one who without giving in to discouragement competently overcomes them. Perseverance in the life of a Christian is a special strength of the spirit, enabling one to achieve goals difficult to attain. Perseverance is manifested when a person puts forth care and effort in pursuing moral good despite difficulties and their inevitable effects of feelings of discouragement. Perseverance is especially evident when the obstacles are long lasting. This is related to stability, which can be termed inflexibility and steadfastness. On the one hand, this spiritual strength guards a person from instability and discouragement due to prolonged trials and, on the other hand, it shields from senseless and spasmodic obstinacy in persisting in what is improper or nonessential.

Salvation is the highest good and final goal of every person. Striving for it, then, ought to be characterized by perseverance. Speaking of the end of times the Lord Jesus announced: "Many will falter then, betraying and hating one another [. . .], because of the increase in evil, the love of most will grow cold. The one who holds out to the end, however, is the one who will see salvation" (Mt. 24:10–12). Hatred, iniquity, and egoism are circumstances which engender discouragement. Nevertheless, St. Paul reminds us that affliction makes for endurance and endurance for tested virtue, and tested virtue for hope that will never disappoint us. All this is the work of the Holy Spirit (*cf.* Rom 5:3–5). Mother Mary Angela understood that through perseverance in the fulfillment of God's will she would realize her vocation. She knew what it meant to love with a love which has no limit to "forbearance [. . .] and its power to endure" (1 Cor 13:7).

From its very beginning the Church always taught that endurance is God's gift which all must strive to attain. The *Catechism of the Catholic Church* reminds us, therefore, that to live, grow, and persevere in the faith until the end, we must nourish it with the Word of God; and we must beg the Lord to increase our faith (*cf.* CCC 162). In another place this same *Catechism* teaches that final perseverance in good works is accomplished with the grace of God (*cf.* CCC 2016). The greater the difficulties which must be overcome, the greater the gift of endurance. Grace is always adequate for the God-given tasks or trials to which one is subjected.

The history of salvation provides examples of situations in which God's help is always proportionate to the need, for instance, in the case of the wrestling Jacob (Gn 32:25–30). In the tradition of the Church the episode of the all-night battle of Jacob with a mysterious "figure", a symbol of a prayerful struggle with God and its victory, is a triumph of perseverance (CCC 2573). Another example is Job, who despite being tempted by his close friends, stood steadfast in faith and received a reward (*cf.* Jas 5:11). Mother Foundress was also subject to trials of all sorts of which the most sorrowful one was, most assuredly, the suppression of the Congregation by the Russians. Then, too, she endured a long-lasting and burdensome illness. Despite this, she never ceased praying and renewing the offering of herself to the Lord.

In the *Act of Consecration to the Sacred Heart of Jesus at the Time of Renewal of Vows*, Mother Mary Angela confirmed her love of the cross of Christ and professed her faith in God's abundant grace. "O Lord, you are mine forever," she prayed on 8 December 1862, "I will never separate myself from you nor from the thorny cross-filled road which leads me to you; I will never fear anything because you are my Light. You will not allow hell to prevail over me; through you I will conquer my enemies because your Heart, which has favored me with so many graces, will always be my refuge" (SW III, 17).

Truly, this was her refuge, especially during her serious illness while concurrently suffering the dark night of her soul. The dark night was as if the last phase in which her Divine Spouse completed the molding of her soul. In his homily on the occasion of her beatification, John Paul II referred to this suffering and stated that Christ "fashioned her soul with great suffering which she accepted with faith and heroic surrender to his will".

The source of her suffering was not only her illness and the many problems related to the management and growth of the Congregation. Her interior difficulties were also the cause of severely intense spiritual suffering. Mother Mary Angela bore them with heroic submission and encouraged her spiritual daughters to do likewise. In a letter to Sister Mary Hedwig she wrote, "The aim of every soul dedicating herself to God should be her sanctification. Do not be disturbed with your failures;

let them humiliate you but not discourage you, because discouragement is a manifestation of self-love and not of the love of God. Remember that for those who love God everything turns out for the good, even failures and imperfections" (SW I, 105).

Mother Foundress' mode of bearing suffering is evidenced in another letter to Sister Mary Hedwig in which she challenges her to perseverance in difficulties in the fulfillment of the will of God: "My dear child, do not yearn even for that consolation which the saints experienced in their sufferings; let your comfort be to suffer without consolation in the greatest abandonment and in imitation of your Divine Spouse, so that with him you may call out: 'It is consummated!' that is, I have fulfilled everything for which I came to religious life—I have fulfilled God's will" (SW I, 106). This is a desire not only to imitate Christ's death on the cross but also to imitate his most perfect fulfillment of the will of his Father.

Significant also are her words suggesting reflection on the reason for entering the Congregation: "Why did I come to a religious community?" This is a realistic question not only for every Felician Sister, but also for every sister and every brother from any religious community. It provokes yet another question, which every believer should ask: "Why am I a Christian?"

Mother Mary Angela knew perfectly well not only why she entered religious life, but also why she founded the Congregation: "to work not only to save oneself but to save others" (SW III, 152). With this perspective of salvation she willingly accepted whatever suffering life did not spare her. The cross, which befell the Foundress of the Felician Sisters, was not a common occurrence for founders of other religious communities. It was an exceptional cross because for almost thirty years (from 20 January 1870) until her death (10 October 1899), in accord with the recommendation of Father Honorat, she effaced herself, avoiding involvement in any major decisions regarding the Congregation. It was due to her illness that the decision to release her from her existing responsibilities was made by Father Honorat on 31 October 1869. Her progressive loss of hearing impeded the fulfillment of a number of responsibilities, specifically those related to her position as superior general. After moving into the newly constructed convent at Smolensk Street in Krakow, she devoted herself to prayer and unobtrusive physical work. She tended garden flowers and decorated the altars where the Blessed Sacrament was exposed and sewed liturgical vestments for neglected and poor churches. At the recommendation of her superiors she took upon herself the editing of the *Constitutions* of the Congregation.

The sufferings of Mother during this time were especially painful. Her experience of the dark night of the soul (1872–1873), which has been already mentioned, intensified her deep feeling of loneliness. Contributing to this was her gradual loss of hearing which hindered her contact with the sisters and later even with her confessor. In such a situation, Mother Foundress could only observe the life and growth of her Congregation as if from a grave. To the end of their lives, most other foundresses, contributed to the formation, development, and renewal of their institutions. However when Mother Mary Angela saw some ventures and initiatives in the Congregation not in accord with her ideals for the Congregation, she could only resort to prayer and acts of mortification. This was an additional cross. This was a further lesson in humility—a lesson in heroic submission to the will of God.

She expressed the state of her soul in one of her letters to Father Honorat: "Confession is the greatest torture for me but, since it cannot be otherwise, I have to accept it in the spirit of penance. I am experiencing terrible interior desolation and heaviness of heart. I feel that only submission to the will of God can make this suffering easier to bear, while prayer can obtain mercy and some strength for me" (SW II/2, 263). The mentioned difficulties she had with confession resulted from her need to communicate with her confessor by written notes. She was deprived, therefore, of any spiritual counsel or words of encouragement. Assuredly, this was a very sorrowful and painful aloneness. This spiritual suffering was increased for her because of a lack of direct contact with the sisters due to her loss of hearing. In this period of her life Mother Mary Angela, in a particular manner, likened herself to Christ who cried from the cross: "My God, my God, why have you forsaken me?" (Mt 27:46).

God accepted the sacrifice of her life and rewarded her suffering. He let her know this while she was yet on earth. One month before her death on 3 September 1899, Bishop John Puzyna handed her the *Apostolic Decree of Approval* of the Congregation. He also gave her a copy of the *Constitutions* of the Congregation together with an approbation for seven years. This was her reward! It is worth mentioning here that very few founders could rejoice over such news during their lifetimes.

PRAYER

Blessed Mary Angela, Foundress of the Congregation of the Felician Sisters
  – pray for us.
Heroic in long-lasting suffering
  – pray for us.
Blessed Mary Angela, to whom God granted the grace of understanding the redeeming value of human suffering
  – pray for us.

[Lord Jesus Christ] *Teach me to suffer with such a love for your Divine will, that I would not choose my own crosses but accept those which you send me;*

that I would not seek relief even for a moment; that I would not even know how to long for heaven, unless you alone, O Lord, fill my heart with this longing.

Teach me to love suffering as you loved the cross; teach me to want to suffer as you desired the cross.

Teach me to suffer with such silence, such purity and such love as your Most Pure Mother suffered. . . (SW III, 14–15).

VIII

LOVE OF THE EUCHARIST

I have asked the Lord that he himself should tell me what I should consider as the greatest grace and from what I will have to give the greatest account. It occurred to me that the Blessed Sacrament is the greatest grace because Jesus in the Blessed Sacrament is the Giver of all graces. He is the source from whom all graces flow. Therefore, it is from the frequent exposition of the Blessed Sacrament and from the daily Holy Communion that we will have to give the most serious account [. . .]. When I think of the future that we might not be allowed to receive daily, I feel much pain. I pity all religious persons who cannot receive Holy Communion as frequently as we do (SW III, 46–47).

It is true that the Blessed Sacrament is the most magnificent gift of God. The Giver of all gifts is present to bestow on us his love, to draw us to himself, and to remind us how dearly he loves us. His presence hidden under the form of bread reminds us that he is the Bread of eternal life. He himself had told us this: "I myself am the Bread of Life. No one who comes to me shall ever be hungry" (Jn 6:35). His desire is that we come to him, and that we nourish ourselves on him. Already in her youthful years, Mother Mary Angela knew that he is the only food she needed to persevere on her chosen path.

In the Eucharistic treatise transmitted to us through St. John, Jesus draws a parallel to the wandering of the Chosen People in the desert (*cf.* Jn 6:32). At that time, the people nourished themselves with manna which was called the bread from heaven (*cf.* Ex 16:4). However, when the fullness of time arrived, we were given more perfect bread from heaven. It is Jesus himself, sent to us by the Father. "It is my Father who gives you the real heavenly bread. God's bread comes down from heaven and gives life to the world" (Jn 6:32, 33). The Giver of life present in the Most Blessed Sacrament is then the gift of the Father, a most sublime gift of the Father, God the Father, who loved the world so much that he gave his only Son (*cf.* Jn 3:16). Therefore, when we adore the Lord Jesus under the form of bread, we adore not only him but also his Father and our Father. The Eucharist opens our eyes to the love of God the Father and to his fatherly care for his adopted sons and daughters.

Mother Mary Angela was fully aware of this beautiful theological truth. In her *Chaplet of Thanksgiving* she specifically thanked God the Father for the love of the Son for us "and especially for the Blessed Sacrament" (SW III, 25). It is very important for today's generation to understand that the Eucharist is a gift of the Heavenly Father. This awakens them to the fact that they are not orphans in this world and that a good and merciful Father stretches out to them a helping hand, which is the loving Heart of Jesus.

Mother Foundress loved the adoration of the Blessed Sacrament. She frequently organized adorations of reparation both during the day as well as in the night. These adorations took place before the tabernacle or while the Blessed Sacrament was exposed in the monstrance. She spent much time and exerted much effort in her endeavors for the privilege of perpetual daily exposition of the most Blessed Sacrament. The privilege was granted by virtue of the *Breve* issued by the Apostolic See on 16 September 1881. This brought her great joy!

To this tremendous happiness, however, was attached the feeling of responsibility for this gift from

God. That is why in the above cited introductory fragment of Mother Mary Angela's meditation, she expresses her fear regarding our accountability for how we use this privilege. In her letter to Father Honorat she complained that this grace of perpetual exposition is not sufficiently appreciated and that there is an inadequate understanding of the spirit of adoration in the Congregation. She adds that the reason for it is because there is no one to enkindle that spirit within the sisters. She requested that Father Honorat help them in this situation (*cf.* SW II/2, 296).

If we truly love another person with our whole heart, then we desire to know everything possible about the loved one. There is a need to know what the beloved is doing at a given moment; how the beloved is feeling; and if the beloved is troubled or worried about anything. Such likewise is the case with God and his creatures. That is why Mary Angela wanted to know as much as was possible about the Blessed Eucharist. In one of her letters she acknowledged that she would like to have practically every book about the Blessed Sacrament. She wrote: "When I hear that a book treats of the Eucharist, a deep desire takes hold of me, and I experience some special interior emotion which sets me afire" (SW II/1, 143). Later, she clarified that her wish to possess all these books was dictated by her search for whatever would arouse in her "a stronger desire for God" (SW II/1, 143).

Mother Foundress eventually gave verbal expression to her immense love for the Eucharistic Lord. To this day it remains as the Felician motto and reads: "*All through the Heart of Mary in honor of the Most Blessed Sacrament*".

Worshipping the Lord Jesus in the Most Blessed Sacrament was always linked by Mother with the hope of obtaining needed graces. When it fell by lot on 13 February 1863, that it was Mother Angela's turn for expiatory adoration, she decided that she would remain before the Blessed Sacrament for all twenty-four hours. She was convinced that if she remained in a position where she would be unseen by others but in the "direct view of the Lord Jesus," he would take pity and look upon her and grant her some spiritual strength. However, if she could not pray, then at least she could gaze at the Lord Jesus and "bask in the warmth of his love" (SW II/1, 127). Mother Angela's very manner of expressing herself gives witness to the sincerity with which she approached the Eucharistic Lord, and reveals her childlike tenderness and trust.

To love the Eucharist is not only to adore the Eucharist. Adoration strengthens and deepens one's interior life when it leads to the full unity which takes place during the reception of Holy Communion. Mary Angela was fully aware of this truth and with her whole heart she desired to receive the Holy Eucharist as often as possible. During her lifetime, however, frequent reception of Communion was not prevalent, but it was permitted. For us, who live during the period of renewal following Vatican Council II, it seems strange that at another time there was a need to request special permission. Religious sisters were able to obtain consent for daily Holy Communion from their confessors. Unfortunately, it did happen in some parishes that local pastors were reluctant to grant this permission. That, in fact, is the reason why in the above cited introductory fragment of Mother's meditation, we can sense her uneasiness in regard to frequent Holy Communion.

Mother Foundress' justification for the frequent reception of Communion was very simple—love. After all, it is evident to everyone, that one who loves desires to be with the beloved. That is how Mary Angela reasoned. In her *Spiritual Counsels* she encouraged Sister Mary Bogdana to receive Holy Communion as frequently as possible because thus "Jesus Christ becomes one with our souls. For that reason we cannot do anything more pleasing to him than to receive him often" (SW III, 112).

In this same manner she encouraged other sisters to frequent Holy Communion. For instance, she explained to Sister Mary Hedwig that the Lord Jesus knows her weakness and has compassion for her, and for that reason, with utmost trust and love, she should offer him her heart as his abode (*cf.* SW I, 93). One, who truly loves the Lord Jesus, unites with him frequently in Holy Communion which strengthens and gives expression to that love. In order that each sister could strengthen her love for Christ and benefit from the fullness of his graces, Mother Angela, in her *Observations on the Constitutions*, advised that the sisters receive daily Holy Communion (*cf.* SW III, 162).

The spiritual daughters of Mother Mary Angela, faithful to the spirit of their Foundress, participate daily in the Eucharistic Liturgy. In the Congregation's *Constitutions*, revised in 1989, in the third chapter which is dedicated to the life of prayer we read: "The Eucharist is the heart of our consecrated life and the focal point of our spiritual heritage" (*Constitutions* III, 55). Article 31 emphatically states that as a community there is daily participation in the celebration of the Eucharistic Sacrifice. The daily exposition of the Blessed Sacrament in the twelve provincial houses of the Congregation offers the opportunity for daily adoration as an expression of love and thanksgiving (*cf. Constitutions* III, 57).

Placing the Eucharist in the center of Felician spirituality is in full accord with the teaching of the Church as expressed in many documents among which is the *Catechism* of John Paul II. It reminds us—in line with the instructions of Vatican Council II—that our Savior instituted the Eucharistic sacrifice of his Body and Blood in order to perpetuate the sacrifice on the cross and to entrust to the Church a memorial of his death and resurrection as "a sacrament of love, a sign of unity, a bond of charity, a Paschal banquet in which Christ is consumed, the mind is filled with grace, and a pledge of future glory is given to us" (CCC 1323).

These various attributes of the Holy Mass serve to demonstrate how inexhaustible are the riches from which each believer can and ought to benefit because the Eucharist is "the source and summit of Christian life" (CCC 1324).

PRAYER

Blessed Mary Angela, Foundress of the Congregation of the Felician Sisters
– pray for us.
Zealous adorer of the Most Blessed Sacrament
– pray for us.
Peaceful and faithful in the most difficult situations
– pray for us.

Lord, I search for you everywhere but I cannot find you even for one second; I do not even recognize you when you come to my heart in Holy Communion.

I do not ask you, Lord, for any consolations. I am even ready to give up feeling your presence during the whole day; however, please do not deprive me of it at the moment when you come into my heart during Holy Communion.

That is my only and constant prayer which I place before you (SW III, 58).

IX

FIDELITY TO THE CHARISM

Love your Congregation dearly. Let its spirit penetrate you deeply. Over and above your father, mother, and everything else in the world, love the will of God so as to be engulfed by it. Because your vocation is readiness for any sacrifice and at any time—serve there where God places you, and always in such way as he points out to you (Modl. 165).

Although the Gospel is one and Christ's Church is the sole one, the teaching of the Gospel can be realized in society in various ways. Some attempt to actualize it by extreme means and others less radically. Some emphasize prayer and contemplation, while others center on apostolic service or works of charity. This then is the rationale for the diversified charisms of the congregations and the differences in their spirituality.

From the very beginning Mother Mary Angela was captivated by the Franciscan spirituality and that is why she was ever watchful that the sisters remain faithful to the ideals of St. Francis of Assisi. She guarded "against the incursion of an alien spirit" (SW I, 49). She recommended that the sisters avail themselves of the spiritual direction of the Capuchin Fathers, obviously, insofar as this was available. She herself remained faithful to Father Honorat, a Capuchin, who was her spiritual director. Adherence to this one spirituality was very prudent because it helped maintain unity in the Congregation and also assisted in the actualization of the particular charism.

Under many aspects, the charism of Mother Mary Angela was similar to the charism of St. Francis. Like him, she attracted sisters who understood her ideal of evangelical life. They had similar life experiences and received a calling as she did. Mother Foundress helped them understand the contemporary needs of the Church and taught them to cooperate with the Holy Spirit in meeting them. Drawing from the experiences of the Capuchin Fathers, she showed the sisters how they could realize the evolving charism. In this manner she was able to achieve a return to the very sources of Christianity, to the original way of actualizing the essential demands of authentic Christian life.

The foundation of the Congregation of the Felician Sisters may very well be considered as that particular time when both Mother Foundress and her sisters discovered and fully grasped the meaning of their charism. Such events, whenever they occur, bring to the light of day and usher into action that which is the very essence of the Gospel. Thus it was that, in the persons of Mary Angela and her spiritual daughters, the Gospel revealed the fullness of its powers in the difficult realities of the times.

An example of the magnetism of this power can be found in the account of a 17 year-old candidate, Rose Wyczalkowska, who decided to join the community of Mary Angela. Her family strongly opposed it. Mother Foundress relates that her father with two other men came and "took the poor girl by force because she refused to go voluntarily. One took her by the head, the other by the legs and then they forcibly put her into the carriage. She shouted so loudly that they gagged her with a handkerchief . . ." (SW II/1, 96). Within a few months, by the strength of her determination, she returned to the Congregation where she remained to the end of her life.

Her powerful determination to be part of the undertaking of Mary Angela can be understood only as a charism granted as a special gift of God. In the theology of a charism we learn that this is a gift which is non-transferable, for it is a gift of the Holy Spirit granted to an individual. This means, that in the case of the above-mentioned Roza, Mary Angela as the Foundress of the Congregation was not bequeathing her charism to Roza, but in reality was helping her to understand her own vocation. Roza, like every Felician Sister, received the charism of the Foundress through the gift of a personal call to the Congregation. She received it through the inspiration of the Holy Spirit as she discovered within herself the desire to do as Mary Angela did and in the same manner as she did. A vocation to the Congregation is exactly such a discovery in oneself of the charism of the Foundress. The same can be said about a vocation to any other congregation. Such an understanding of a vocation emphasizes the dignity of the person called. For this is a personal calling, a call by name (*cf.* 1 Sm 3:10).

Even now, long after the death of the Foundress, the charism of the Congregation is transmitted together with the grace of a vocation. That is why those who are called ought discern and deepen the understanding of their personal charism through actual acquaintance with the life and work of Mother Mary Angela. Such information is available through conferences and written materials on the topic, through discussions with the sisters, and the witness of the lives of the sisters. This is the first phase. The second is undoubtedly acquaintance with the actual experience of the daily life of the Congregation, its customs and pious practices, and its apostolic ministry. Such a discernment of the personal charism takes place during the postulancy and the novitiate phases of religious life.

Mother Angela uncovered her charism in action. She gathered poor abandoned children and homeless elderly women. She bowed in deference to their adversities and was solicitous to bring them help with her available means. No private revelation or theoretical inquiry led her to an understanding of her charism, but it was her openness to the voice of God in her heart and the practical assistance she extended to the needy. Her charism expressed itself in spontaneous works of mercy and in educational and cultural activities. The spirit of Franciscan poverty deeply penetrated her total activity. Her apostolic service was characterized by a fervent love for the mystery of Christ in the Eucharist and the imitation of the Mother of God in her obedience to the will of God.

Obedience to the will of God was the most important standard for her behavior. The will of her superiors was a manifestation of the will of God, which explains the characteristic trait of her charism, a childlike obedience to the Church. Fulfilling the will of God, Mary Angela led a "consecrated" life. This demanded the sacrifice of spiritual preferences to which would belong, for example, the desire for the contemplative life. She sacrificed the contemplative life to serve others in their particular needs.

During the times when the enemies of the Church openly attacked and when poverty, ignorance, and immorality blocked the way to God, the charism of Mary Angela showed itself to be efficacious not only for the Church but also for her country. Charism is a gift to be used for the benefit of the Church. The existing circumstances of the time and place determine the specifics for which it is to be utilized for the special needs of the Church. These are conditioned historically so that the charism evolves as it serves the actual needs of the Church. Such is Mary Angela's charism!

Mary Angela's charism became more defined because of her openness in responding to the existing needs of the Church. She constantly sought to perfect the means for its realization. In her search, however, she remained ever faithful to the spirit of St. Francis. That is why she wrote to Father Honorat: "Perhaps it is a manifestation of God's will toward us that our Lord does not want the *Constitutions* to be anybody's work but yours, Father, so that no other spirit even the holiest, should permeate it [. . .], I feel in no way inclined to submit your work to the judgment of another priest. After all, he does not know the spirit of our Congregation and God did not designate him to write our *Constitutions*" (SW II/2, 76; *cf.* 77).

It happened once that a very influential diocesan priest, who was not a religious, "seriously undertook" the spiritual direction of the sisters at a local home. Mother Foundress objected categorically to this, because she did not want to be responsible "for confused consciences and temptations" and she feared that there would follow "a complete spiritual dissent from the Motherhouse" (SW II/1, 206, 207).

Mother Foundress presented a brief but meaningful description of the spirit of the Congregation to Sister Hedwig: "As to our spirit, you know it well: self-denial, obedience, poverty, work, and dedication for others without regard for oneself" (SW I, 91). Whenever she noticed a weakening of this spirit she grieved deeply.

In another letter, ten years later, she complained to Mother Mary Anna: "The spirit grows weaker and greater weariness overtakes us not only at prayer but also in dedication. And why should this be so? Ours is a seraphic spirit which is different from that of other communities and which can be nurtured only with self-denial and prayer" (SW I, 48). If in her own lifetime Mother Angela felt "weariness" set in, so what can be said about the spirit of the Congregation after more than a hundred years of its existence? Nevertheless, she not only states the problem but provides the remedial measures for it, namely, self-denial and prayer.

Periodical weakening of the spirit which, after all, is a natural phenomenon in the life of any congregation gives rise to the temptation of "introducing another spirit" different than that of a foundress. This is the temptation of seeking a new way of renewal which Mother Foundress would reject. Renewal in another spirit would change the identity of the Congregation. Such a situation, however, could possibly occur should the needs of the Church, which formerly had been the basis of the Congregation's charism, no longer exist. The following, however, remain actual. The poor are always among us. Defense against religious ignorance and immorality is needed today more than ever. If some "weariness of spirit" is recognized, then the most effective means for renewal is self-denial and prayer.

A continual renewal of spirit is possible, and even necessary, because the Congregation of Mary Angela possesses the essential traits of a charismatic movement. Its charismatic character manifests itself most forcefully whenever its apostolic service is dynamic, its dedication most visible, and its oneness of spirit undoubted.

The concern of Mother Mary Angela for preserving the seraphic spirit among her sisters is a beautiful example for persons who are not members of her Congregation. Her approach to the matter can serve as an ideal for all who wish to benefit from spiritual direction; for instance, such as is offered by their confessors who are able to give them detailed directives to help them in their pursuit of perfection.

The laity when deciding to profit from this direction should first consider which spirituality is more appealing: Franciscan, Carmelite or Ignatian. After reaching a decision, one ought to remain loyal to a chosen director, provided that no objectively determined impediments exist. It is important to remember this, especially when after a certain time of spiritual guidance, doubts occur if what one is experiencing is not what one expected. A change of spiritual director in such a situation would not be helpful on the way to perfection and could even prove harmful, all the more if there already had been repeated changes.

Mother Mary Angela remained faithful to her director, Father Honorat, even though it is known that at times relating with him was not easy (*cf.* SW II/2, 34).

PRAYER

A ready submission to God's will
   – obtain for us, Mary Angela.
A generous spirit of dedication to the sick and needy
   – obtain for us, Mary Angela.
Numerous and self-sacrificing vocations to your Congregation
   – obtain for us, Mary Angela.

I cry out to you and beg you, please show yourself to me for at least a while. I keep asking you—what is it that you want of me [. . .].

You know, O Lord, because you read my heart, that I am not tired of serving you; that I would not leave you for all the treasures and pleasures of the world; that I do not even have such temptations; that I do not have any regrets leaving anything for you, unless, that I did not have more to offer you (SW III, 30).

X

INTERIOR LIFE

I recommend as your main practice and as a special intention in your prayers: that you may never desire anything else but that which God wants and that you accept everything from him with the conviction that what he sends you is the best for your soul, even if it appears difficult and painful or actually harmful (SW I, 97–98).

The interior life of every person is a seemingly inscrutable matter, undisclosed to others, although it is possible that it can be revealed to others in confidence. In the case of a person like Mother Mary Angela we can learn something about her from her letters and the various notes and prayers she wrote on different occasions. It is significant and valuable to know about her interior life because it allows us to benefit from her experiences and to emulate her. The few observations presented here do not reveal the total riches of Mother Angela's interior life. They serve only to spur us on to seek a fuller acquaintance with her spiritual profile.

Love of God was most important in the interior life of Mother Mary Angela. It was this she totally yearned for and prayed for most fervently because—as she herself wrote—"If I had the love of God, I would possess everything because to the one who loves, everything turns out for the good" (SW II/1, 38). This in no way indicates that Mother Mary Angela did not actually have this love of God. She certainly did possess it but it is characteristic of love that it is never enough. She desired to love God above all and continually to perfect that love. Her aspirations for a yet more perfect love became the cause of her personal feelings of dissatisfaction with herself. This, however, was the driving force as she traveled the road toward interior perfection.

The yearning for an always greater love of God was an outgrowth of her deep faith. Here we are not concerned only with the faith whose essence is the truths revealed and taught by the Church but, more so, the faith in God's constant presence in the daily life of Mother Foundress and her sisters. Her efforts in spiritual growth and apostolic ministry created many difficulties which Mary Angela always looked upon through the prism of faith. She perceived in these the will of God or she tried to find in them some sign from God. As an example, she greatly desired to pronounce her vows on the feast of the Presentation of the Blessed Virgin Mary because she treasured that day and always looked upon it as the founding day of the Congregation. She waited for the written permission from Father Honorat. Unfortunately, the letter which contained this permission arrived after the desired date and she did not pronounce her vows. She accepted this as the will of God: "God's ways are strange. Practically each of my desires is almost always crossed" (SW II/2, 32). Such an attitude is an expression of great humility and faith in the Providence of God. A person without such faith would have looked at it as normal "human coincidence" of no importance to anyone. However, for Mother these were the occasions which "crossed out her own desires" and which she renounced, even those which in every other respect appeared as good.

The quoted example reveals readiness for spiritual suffering which in interior life functions as a purifying agent. Worthy of note here is her complaint about her inability to bear sufferings, including those which resulted from her hearing handicap. "This sickness"—she wrote to Father Honorat—"not only drains me physically but it drives me to complete spiritual depression. I suffer interiorly a thousand times more than physically since I do not know how to suffer for Jesus . . . " (SW II/2, 14).

Mother Mary Angela was totally aware that one must learn to bear suffering with great patience. Her life is witness to the fact that it can be learned and that it also can become the road to holiness.

On the path to perfection there appear not only physical but also spiritual sufferings which result from the inability to achieve one's good intentions. Such internal experiences may also be the source of a variety of temptations or their consequences. As an example, not knowing how to accept suffering may result in a temptation to yield and to give up. It happens often that a person desiring a more perfect interior life undergoes trials. It is possible that Satan, displeased with some evident spiritual progress, wants to lead the person astray, just as he tried to do with Jesus in the desert. At that point an internal battle ensues. As a rule, the battle is very difficult because the temptation takes on the semblance of something good. In this situation, prayer to the Holy Spirit can assure victory by inspiring one to respond according to the will of God.

Mother Mary Angela likens the battle with temptations to withstanding a storm. In her *Spiritual Counsels* to Sister Mary Bogdana she wrote: "When fierce storms arise, let us not draw back but let us fight all the more against the flesh, the world, and the devil. The greater the struggle, the more splendid the wreath; the greater the persecution of the tempter, the more glorious the virtue of the sufferer" (SW III, 125).

Mother Mary Angela refers here to three sources of temptation: our own bodies, our surroundings, and Satan. Thus, there is a constant need of vigilance and a resolute determination to fight, so as not to be taken unaware or be vanquished by the temptation.

She fortified Sister Mary Bogdana with these words: "We are surrounded on all sides by temptations; however, let us not despair but let us pray and cry out to Christ [. . .], perhaps God is trying us out in small things to determine whether we really love him . . ." (SW III, 125). Such a struggle is necessary for anyone aspiring to perfection, just as training is important for the athlete who is preparing for participation in a sporting event. (*cf.* 1 Cor 9:24–27).

The battle with temptations allows us also to know ourselves better: to understand our inclinations, weaknesses, and faults. Knowing ourselves is a basic element in striving for perfection. Just as knowledge of the laws of nature allows us to be prepared for any contingency and to subdue the earth (*cf.* Gn 1:28), so likewise the knowledge of our own nature allows us to predict our reactions and to have better control over ourselves. Skill in this control is necessary for spiritual progress.

Mother Mary Angela sincerely desired to know herself as well as possible and she prayed for this gift which she was convinced comes from the Holy Spirit. In the meditation about the *Model Religious* she makes mention of such a prayer: "I asked Jesus to help me recognize the evil which is in me" (SW III, 53). At the conclusion of this meditation she describes the condition of her soul, from which it can be seen that she really knew herself well. She humbly confesses: "I find it so difficult to mortify myself and yet I know that it is the violent who lay hold of heaven" (SW III, 55). Obviously, however, her longing to "lay hold of heaven" was more powerful than all her earthly weaknesses. Today Mother Foundress rejoices with the splendor of the redeemed, as the blessed one; and for us she left a beautiful example of the "violent" and, at the same time, of an unusually quiet, patient, and untiring struggle for heaven.

The constant combat with one's weaknesses and the practice of virtue, which is the striving for personal interior growth, entails effort. At times, it calls for very much effort, especially if one's faults are deeply rooted, and the circumstances of life are exceptionally hostile.

One who desires to progress in this struggle for interior growth must place many demands on oneself. On that score, Mother Mary Angela did not spare herself in the least. For instance, she very energetically struggled to overcome her pride and egoism. She confessed to her spiritual director, Father Honorat: "I consider your admonition as just. I know that I deserved a more severe reproof because there is so much pride in me that it shows up in everything I do." Later she added: "As a matter of fact, when I began writing to you, I used to feel hurt at first, even though I did not like myself for it. All of that is in the past, for although there is much pride in me, your admonitions are wiping it off" (SW II/2, 103–104). Anyone who ever tried to "wipe off" pride knows how painful and endless this process is.

She struggled to root out her faults by setting severe demands on herself. As an example, she always attempted to conscientiously participate in all common spiritual exercises with the sisters. In rendering an account of this to Father Honorat, she confessed that she tries to fulfill her spiritual exercises very faithfully, but she is not satisfied with herself. Consequently she desired to fulfill them with an even greater interior devotion (*cf.* SW II/2, 213).

Mother Foundress was very well aware of the fact that zeal in striving for perfection was also a gift of God. And so she prayed: "O Lord, have mercy on me and force me to do what I ought to do. Give me simplicity of disposition towards my spiritual director. Perhaps a constant openness, even in small matters, will enable me to remain in control of myself" (SW III, 60). From this prayer flow two counsels in regard to interior life: constant vigilance over oneself and obedience to the spiritual director.

Spiritual direction is indispensable in interior life. It does not limit itself only to the guidance of a regular confessor, nor is it necessary that it be connected with the sacrament of penance. In Church tradition this takes place when three conditions are met. First, the spiritual director should have experience in spiritual matters; then he must exercise prudence in making decisions; and he must have a profound knowledge of all the aspects of theology. Secondly, a director is freely chosen by a person who, in turn, makes a commitment to accept direction with trust in the guidance which is offered. Finally, a person who is seeking a director ought to do so only because of a desire for a life of perfection according to the Gospel.

Mother Mary Angela desired nothing as much as this perfect living of the Gospel. In seeking a spiritual director for herself, she found what she desired in Father Honorat. She trusted him completely and was obedient to his directives and his admonitions. The fact that he was beatified confirms that he was a director of profound spiritual knowledge. Anyone wishing to become familiar with his uncommon guidance is directed to the clear-sighted letters of Mary Angela to Father Honorat (*cf.* SW II/1, 2). Obviously, spiritual direction is not restricted only for persons consecrated to the exclusive service of God. Everyone who wishes to live the Gospel more fully is encouraged to benefit from spiritual direction.

Mother Foundress realized that having the opportunity of receiving spiritual direction is a gift from God. She thanked God for this grace of a deeper knowledge of her soul's wretchedness through the guidance of Father Honorat (*cf.* SW II/2, 212). This motivated her to strive even more zealously in her pursuit of perfection. The way in which she did this was, among others, the practice of making resolutions and then rendering an account of her progress. Thanks to this practice, Mother was able to receive observations regarding her continued progress in her spiritual life. In one letter she very directly wrote that she wishes to give a regular monthly account and requests that Father Honorat likewise respond regularly. His letters and his counsels were an encouragement for her spiritual efforts (*cf.* SW II/2, 233).

It goes without saying that if spiritual direction is to be effective it must be based on trust and sincerity. However, it may happen that despite the fact that there is sincerity, there may arise some sort of misunderstanding. This cannot constitute a reason for ceasing further direction. Such situations also arose in the spiritual life of Mother Angela and this is evident from her words written to Father Honorat: "I try to be sincere with you, even down to the smallest detail, all the more when it concerns a serious matter. When my vocation is at stake, would I be a hypocrite and pay attention to human respect?" (SW II/1, 55).

Mother Foundress remained faithful to her spiritual director even when it seemed to her that his method of guiding her was harsh and his counsels awakened interior resistance. In spite of this, she faithfully followed his recommendations (*cf.* SW II/1, 196). To admit something like this to one's director is unquestionably an expression of humility and trust, and at the same time it helped to overcome the difficulties she experienced.

The advice to avoid aspiring to experiences of extraordinary phenomena is very valuable for one's interior life. Mother Foundress was convinced that such aspirations in religious life are dangerous. She feared this because "it makes religious life and dedication for others very difficult" (SW II/1, 154). In one of her letters to Father Honorat in which she speaks of the spiritual state of one of the sisters, Mother clarifies her reasons for this. She decided to "guard her from all exceptions" like remaining in constant prayer as a victim soul, and also demanding that she lead "an ordinary life in an extraordinary way," because—as she justifiably observed—"extraordinary phenomena together with spiritual pride can work on one's imagination" (SW II/1, 186–187).

Extraordinary behavior in spiritual life is very dangerous because instead of leading to union with God, it tends to lead to centering on oneself. Also very harmful and perilous is spiritual pride which puffs up self-satisfaction with one's own humility and progress in perfection. Mother Mary Angela chose another path of logic regarding the spiritual life: live an ordinary life in an extraordinary way. Accordingly, she never yearned for any private revelations.

The aspects of the interior life presented above by Mary Angela indicate that these are the keystone or foundation of her whole life. Her rich interior life was the source of her zeal in her apostolic services and in her sacrificial dedication for the salvation of others.

In no way is it possible in this short reflective reading to portray the tremendous richness of the spiritual life of Mother Foundress. She was constantly concerned about her growth in perfection and she employed such methods as the examination of conscience, meditation, retreats, common and private prayers, particularly adoration of the Blessed Sacrament, mortification, and physical work. Her spiritual life is a beautiful example of perseverance in striving for perfection. She is truly an excellent spiritual director not only for her spiritual daughters, but also for anyone who wishes to live the fullness of the Gospel.

PRAYER

Excellent spiritual director
   – pray for us.
A living faith
   – obtain for us, Mary Angela.
A pure love of God,
   – obtain for us, Mary Angela.

Father, accept the offering I make of myself to you and involve me in the work for the salvation of the world.

Give me a heart overflowing with love, great humility, and firm hope so that I might witness to Jesus in the world.

As I abide in Jesus and the heart of his Mother, I offer you thanks for granting my request and I humbly ask for protection from all dangers (Modl. 164).

XI

SERVICE OF A RELIGIOUS SUPERIOR

Since I bear the title of Mother, I should have the heart of a mother; I am even more obligated to do this than any other superior, yet I think that the worst stepmother would not behave as I do. I really admire the humility of our sisters. If anyone treated me only once the way I treat them, I think I would become estranged towards them and perhaps even hate them. I should be concerned about every sister in the Congregation because I will have to give an account before God for each one (SW III, 43).

The topic of leadership is a sensitive one, especially in religious congregations. It can be considered and profitably discussed only within a milieu where those involved have a sense of responsibility for the unity of a community and also have a great respect and love for the leaders and for those being led.

The matter of authority always evokes strong feelings. It is a difficult matter to begin with, because the decisions of a superior are an expression of the will of God in any given community. They are the result of the cooperation of a human will and the will of God. The subject of leadership is also sensitive because the decisions of a superior often may relate to matters of conscience or matters concerned with the spiritual life of the religious sisters and brothers.

In general, such an understanding of authority in religious congregations and in the Church demands faith in the providence of God operating through human individuals. The effort to fathom the will of

God and that of individuals may lead to difficulties and problems at times, due to a strong over involvement of the human will. The difficulty in accepting the will of superiors can also arise from the fact that, after all, superiors do not receive any private revelations, but undertake their decisions on the basis of discerning related circumstances. The will of God reveals itself in events and the task of superiors is to discern these events and transmit them into definite decisions.

Mother Mary Angela always desired to do the will of God most perfectly, so she continually strove to discern it honestly. She frequently reflected whether what she considered as the will of God for herself or for the Congregation was truly the will of God. Therefore, she would resort to her spiritual director, Father Honorat, to help her in discerning it. For example, in reference to the future of the Congregation, she wrote: "Father, I leave to you the discernment of God's will in it, since his will should be revealed to you and not to me and be given through you to be made known to us. It behooves us only to fulfill whatever you, Father, recognize as God's will" (SW II/2, 56–57).

Since for a long period of time Mother Foundress had lived as an "ordinary" sister, obediently submissive to the rigors of religious life in a community of which, after all, she herself was the Foundress, her method of discharging the function of a superior is unusually instructive. For instance, disclosing to her superior the state of her interior life demonstrates her great humility and surrender to God's will in the least detail. Mother Mary Angela knew not only how to be a superior; she also knew how to obey one.

Mother Foundress understood her role as superior as that of fulfilling the will of God and being of service to the sisters. She considered that her function was "to serve as a superior" and that it was a "dangerous position" for her (*cf.* SW III, 18), undoubtedly, because she feared to succumb to the sin of pride in having been selected above others. Consequently, after her election as a superior in 1864, and somewhat like Solomon in his prayer for wisdom in judgment (*cf.* 1 Kgs 3:7-9), she prayed intensely and fervently for this wisdom and all necessary graces. In this prayer she begged for the necessary courage to inflame the indifferent sisters, to awaken the slothful ones, to help the wayward, and "to increase the fervor of the devoted" (SW III, 19). In conclusion, she prayed that through her service God himself would be the superior of the Congregation: "[Omnipotent God], since I accepted this position because you wished it, I implore your mercy and beg you to be the superior of this religious community and rule over it through me as a father over his family and a good shepherd over his flock" (SW III, 19). This prayer clearly relates to the words of the Lord Jesus about the Good Shepherd (*cf.* Jn 10:11).

The very substance of Mary Angela's prayer for a proper fulfillment of her "service of leadership" demonstrates that she felt responsible not only for the "external" activities of the Congregation, that is, the accomplishment of the undertaken ministries in the world, but also for its spiritual life, as evidenced in the interior life of each sister.

In a letter to Sister Mary Aniela she wrote: "I always desire your sanctity. I constantly commend you to Jesus in my unworthy prayers" (SW I, 25). To Sister Mary Hedwig she wrote joyfully: "I am happy to note that your external activity is based upon and flows from your interior life" (SW I, 88). Such words of praise from her superior most certainly strengthened Sister Hedwig in spirit and encouraged her to face future struggles.

Here, it is worth noting the concern which Mother Mary Angela felt about the authenticity of the life of her spiritual daughters: the balance of interior life with apostolic service. Keeping the proper harmony is not exactly easy. After all, further in that same letter, Mother reminded Sister Mary Hedwig, that while leading others to salvation, a sister should not neglect her own spiritual progress.

A good example of Mother Foundress' solicitude for the sisters as well as for their spiritual development and their health is contained in another letter to Sister Hedwig. Again and again she reminded her as a superior, "that in giving themselves to others they do not cease to strive for their own spiritual progress" (SW I, 147). On this occasion she admonished her not to overdo the mortifications and nightly watches at prayer. She even told her to write shorter letters so as not to stay up too late at night.

Among these reminders, there is also an apparently simple but very prudent counsel: "I do not excuse you from the afternoon snack and I encourage you to conserve your health, but not to pamper yourself, so that you can serve God more perfectly" (SW I, 148). This is truly motherly advice—take care of your health! But the motivation is on target—to be able to serve God better. This sincere concern was Mother's response to the genuine sincerity of Sister Mary Hedwig. Here also, authority and obedience manifest themselves as a sign of a deep love flowing from the love of God.

It is worth to indicate the importance of the primacy of love in the exercise of authority. Mother Foundress was well aware that there can be something in a person which could be termed a "hunger for power" and the use of power by that individual can be detrimental to the possibility of personal spiritual growth (*cf.* SW III, 210). Consequently, in the *Observations on the Constitutions* she included this meaningful comment: "It seems to me that, especially at the Centers, there should be one authority—the authority of communal love" (SW III, 210). "One authority of communal love" is the strongest foundation of authority and obedience. The primacy of love so stated is most consonant with the will of Jesus Christ, who when entrusting the authority of the keys to St. Peter asked him, as much as, three times: "Simon, son of John, do you love me more than these others?" (Jn 21:15). When Peter affirmed this, Jesus entrusted to him the authority over his sheepfold: "Tend my sheep" (Jn 21:16).

The desire to exercise authority in one's community does not necessarily have to be dictated by self-love. A person can be convinced that there is a better way to lead in the community, or that something needs to be changed for the greater good. In the light of the dialog between Jesus and Peter there is no other way, but to love more than the others do. When the Lord Jesus sees this, he himself will see to it that this person is entrusted with the responsibility. If authority is to come from the will of God, let it remain thus to the end; for it is not right to try to constrain the Lord Jesus in any way to entrust it to this or that person.

Many may deem it an easy task to fulfill the service of a superior. However, to be a good superior demands, above all, patience and humility. St. Francis draws attention to this in his *Admonitions*: "We can never tell how patient or humble a person is when everything is going well with him. But when those who should cooperate with him do the exact opposite, then we can tell. A man has as much patience and humility as he has then, and no more" (Writings II, 83). Thus, well-done service in leadership can be a way to perfection.

In order to help the superiors in the Congregation in this task of leadership, Mother Foundress formulated an excellent *Examination of Conscience for Superiors* (SW III, 173–176). The first question in the *Examination* refers to the love for those whom they lead, since for these sisters that should represent God's love for them. The second question directs attention to the Good Shepherd, who gave his life for his sheep. For the superior, this self-giving can be manifested in sacrificing comforts, personal advantages, time, and work. In another question she directs them to examine their attitudes toward sisters who show no special talents. Are they ignored by the superior and thus disdained by the others? In such situations Mother quotes the words of the Gospel: "People who are in good health do not need a doctor; sick people do" (Mt 9:12), and that the Good Shepherd carries the sick lamb in his arms. A superior ought to imitate the Good Shepherd.

The subsequent question calls attention to the superior's obligation to provide for the needs of the sisters, so that, in desiring to satisfy these needs the sisters would not be tempted to transgress their vow of obedience. She exhorts them to reflect: "Does she console them, visit them and even anticipate their needs in her concern about their temptations and spiritual difficulties?" (SW III, 174). Other questions refer to equal treatment of the sisters, the manner of conducting her office, and the courage necessary in reprimanding them. Finally, and this is exceptionally noteworthy, she asks about self-reliance in reaching decisions. Mother Angela is convinced that "it is indeed very difficult to be obedient to superiors who do not conduct themselves according to their own reasoning or the spirit of God but allow themselves to be influenced by another person and blindly follow her inclinations" (SW III, 176). It is evident here that the proper fulfillment of the responsibilities of a superior facilitates obedience.

Whatever Mother Angela included in the *Examination of Conscience*, she herself practiced as a superior. Her concern for the sick sisters deserves special attention. It was particularly to them that she wanted to be a true mother, sister, and friend as well as all that they had left in the world and which could have brought them comfort in their illness (*cf.* SW III, 174).

From the various accounts about Mother Mary Angela, it is known that she used to travel to visit seriously ill or dying sisters. For instance, when Sister Mary Juniper, serving at a Center in Ges was grievously ill with brain fever, Mother went to visit her despite the fact that this entailed an arduous three-day journey by horse and carriage. Later, Sister Mary Juniper wrote to Father Honorat, "O my God, Jesus almost resurrected me. Now I am still very weak, but every word and every look of Mother Angela, as everyone can see, has had a truly miraculous healing effect upon me. My Father, only God knows what is going on with me because of her visit" (A. Gorski, *Angela Truszkowska*, Poznan 1959, p. 168, *cf.* p. 253).

Not only had the directives for servant leadership come from the personal experiences of Mother Angela, but as was mentioned on other occasions, there was also the teaching of obedience in the example of her own life as an "ordinary" sister following the commands and wishes of the Congregation's superiors. She wrote about this topic: "I understand that obedience is not only external but it requires the submission of reason" (SW II/2, 256). Such submission of reason can only be developed in oneself by personal efforts.

Reason and common sense in her understanding of obedience referred chiefly to the possibilities of the realization of assigned duties. When Mary Angela became very ill with her loss of hearing and it was difficult for her to communicate with the sisters, she pleaded to be freed from her service as a superior. As Father Honorat delayed his decision she insisted, explaining that it was hard for her to believe that it was the will of God that she remain a superior when God deprived her of the faculty which is indispensable for this office (*cf.* SW II/2, 12). Mother Foundress was adamant about not assuming duties that she would not be able to perform well. She also cautioned the sisters about the same.

From this example, it follows, that obedience should not only be the "submission of reason," but also that common sense should govern the assigning of duties which a person is capable of performing well.

This, obviously, requires not only prudence on the part of superiors, but also proper discernment of the possibilities of the sisters, together with their God-given abilities and talents. Conversely, knowledge about these qualities of the sisters also depends upon their sincerity toward superiors.

The ability to perform well in one's assigned tasks engenders peace of conscience, strengthens trust in superiors, and increases zeal in discharging new assignments. The sense of satisfaction from knowing that a duty has been executed well is a positive factor for self-improvement. That is why words of acknowledgment on the part of superiors are not meaningless but do carry great value and add to this feeling of interior peace and fulfillment. In the final analysis, the foundation of all this is love, which unites a community and governs it as one—"one authority bonded by common love".

The example cited above of Mother Mary Angela's request to resign from the responsibilities of a superior helps us to realize how totally she desired to fulfill the will of God and only God. After all, as a Foundress, she could have tendered her resignation and directed the sisters to select someone else. However, she wanted to remain obedient to the end and until she was dispensed, she discharged her duties despite great physical suffering and spiritual trials.

This attitude arose from her deep conviction that in obeying her superiors she was also obeying God (*cf.* SW I, 97). She wanted to do nothing of her own will. Her example demonstrates that in a community no one should arbitrarily free oneself from assigned duties. If a person cannot cope with these, a request to be released can be presented. The Lord Jesus did not come down from the cross—he was removed.

These directives of Mother Mary Angela related to the service of a leader are valuable not only for religious. They can also benefit the laity in their daily lives. After all, almost all of us are in some dependent relationship with others even though one is possibly "in charge": at work, in school, or in the family. Actually here, authority is not understood as a sign of the will of God, but it is essential for the common good. Concern about the common good is an expression of the love of neighbor. Within lay organizations, relations between the leader and the members should be based upon the love of neighbor.

It is the will of God that all Christians exercising leadership roles should be mindful of this obligation to love those over whom they are in charge.

PRAYER

A spirit of humility
   – obtain for us, Mary Angela.
A Christlike view of everyone and everything
   – obtain for us, Mary Angela.
A spirit of service and love for the Church
   – obtain for us, Mary Angela.

Allow me [Lord], to love others for your sake. Since you placed me in this position, allow me to perform my duties towards them. After all, you did not commit your flock to Peter until you assured yourself that he had love in his heart.

Why did you leave me in this position when you saw that there was no love in my heart? Is it because you wanted me to feel its burden all the more; that a greater responsibility awaited me? I do not beg this relief for myself but for others. Inspire within me this love of neighbor or take me out of this office (SW III, 45).

XII

DEVOTION TO THE MOTHER OF GOD

Just as Jesus pointed out the Blessed Virgin to John from the cross saying: "There is your Mother," so I too, taking leave of you, say the same words. I commit you to her care and place you in her Immaculate Heart. May she protect you all the days of your life until she leads you to the feet of Jesus. Go to her with all your cares; seek her counsel in all your doubts and consolation in your sufferings. Let her take the place of everyone and everything in your life (SW III, 113).

The above-quoted words of spiritual counsel to an unknown sister provide us with a mere suggestion of all the love and confidence which Mary Angela showered upon the Mother of God from the beginning. Her exceptionally warm bond with Mary began already in her childhood. Concerned about the health of their eldest daughter, her parents entrusted her to the care of the Immaculate Mother who, in turn, took care not only of Sophia's health but drew her so completely to herself that she became Sophia's ideal for everything in her life. She became her model of perfection in humility, silence, obedience, and patience. When Mary Angela became convinced of her vocation and began gathering her spiritual daughters together, she learned maternal love from Mary. She truly wanted to be a real mother to each of her sisters. In one of her meditations she reproached herself that in her dealings with them she was unpleasant, harsh, and unapproachable. Whereas, "since I bear the title of Mother,"—she wrote—"I should have the heart of a mother . . . " (SW III, 43).

However, what she most earnestly desired to learn from the Mother of God was to perfectly carry out the will of God. Mary's "let it be done to me" was for Mary Angela the ideal of obedience to God and for that reason she constantly sought to discern what the will of God was for her, and then strove to fulfill it perfectly. In teaching her sisters obedience to the will of God, it was specifically Mary whom she gave as a model to follow. On the day before the feast of the Holy Name of Mary, she prayed that all the sisters would faithfully imitate Mary, and to Sister Hedwig she forwarded the following wishes: "that you imitate Mary in everything, especially in her love of God and all people, in her willing and prompt fulfilling of the will of God, and in the courageous carrying of the cross not for one day only but throughout your whole life" (SW I, 126).

She likewise encouraged another sister not to seek spiritual consolation as she daily carried her cross, but rather to repeat constantly with Mary: "Behold the handmaid of the Lord, be it done to me according to your will, O my Jesus" (SW I, 155).

Mother Angela intensified her love and union with Mary through frequent repetition of acts of placing herself in Mary's care. Her renewal of vows before the picture of Our Lady of Czestochowa deserves particular mention. Without doubt she also entrusted the sisters to the Mother of God and encouraged them personally to make this act of love. In her letters to the sisters we often find this or similar closings: "I commend you to the Hearts of Jesus and Mary . . . " (cf. SW I, 153).

A letter to Father Honorat in which Mother Mary Angela details some specifics of her devotion to Our Lady of Czestochowa testifies to her particular veneration of the Czestochowa icon. She mentions the fact that she had prayed for the preservation of the Congregation even before the dispersion by the police and her prayer was heard. She prayed also for the permission for the privilege of the Exposition of the Blessed Sacrament, and again her prayer was heard. It is for these reasons that she chose Our Lady of Czestochowa as the Superior of the Congregation and placed the insignia of her authority before her image. "That picture"—she wrote—"was a witness to our dedicated life of service to others [. . .]. To me it is so very precious! My greatest desire is to pray before it again and to make my vows before it" (SW II/1, 292).

This picture remains to this very day in the Congregation. It is deeply cherished by the sisters not only because it portrays their highest Superior, but also because it reminds them of their Mother Foundress and of her great love for Mary, the Queen of Poland.

This great love found expression also in her efforts to spread the cult of the Mother of God. In the *Spiritual Counsels* to Sister Mary Bogdana, Mother Angela asked her to especially have a deep devotion to the Blessed Virgin and to encourage others to this devotion also, because those who place their trust in her may be sure of salvation (*cf.* SW III, 117). Mother rejoiced greatly whenever the sisters went to Czestochowa to pray at Jasna Gora for the intentions of the Congregation and their country. She was happy about their participation in the devotions in the Sanctuary, and also because of the solemnity and beauty of the liturgy (*cf.* SW II/1, 73, 103).

Mary Angela managed to realize her desire of spreading devotion to the Blessed Mother by distributing medals and making the Chaplet to the Immaculate Heart of Mary widely accepted. Occasionally, she requested Father Honorat to bless these medals and chaplets (*cf.* SW II/1, 70, 81). In one of her letters to him she told him of the great devotion which she had to the Immaculate Heart of Mary. "Today, while I was reciting the chaplet to the Immaculate Heart of Mary," —she wrote—"I felt a strong urge to propagate this devotion at least in our Congregation" (SW II/1, 81). A copy of the text for the chaplet was brought from

France and Mother had it translated. She herself also threaded the beads for these chaplets, having in mind to distribute them to her sisters and those persons who came to the Centers (*cf.* SW II/1, 81).

Through this devotion to the Heart of Mary, Mother Foundress desired to express her love for the Mother of the Savior and to reciprocate Mary's love for all people. The heart was and is the symbol of love, tenderness, and kindness. Designating the Heart of Mary as the Immaculate Heart of Mary even more strongly accentuated the impeccability and purity of Mary's love for us. She loves us without even waiting for our acknowledgment, for our veneration, or our gestures of honor.

It was this kind of love that Mother Mary Angela desired to learn; with this kind of love she wanted to gift her sisters, her spiritual daughters. Trusting that they would always preserve in their hearts the memory of the Immaculate Mother's love for them, she promulgated the motto "All through the Heart of Mary." Later the second phrase was added: "in honor of the Most Blessed Sacrament." Thus originated the motto which to this day is in use by the Congregation of the Felician Sisters.

This beautiful motto reminds the sisters of the great devotion that Mother had to the Heart of Mary and to the Eucharistic Lord. It calls to mind the truth that Mary is the Mediatrix leading us to the Lord Jesus, and also that his constant and redeeming presence is among us under the appearance of bread. This example of Mother Foundress, as well as her recommendations relative to the devotion to Mary, became extremely vital elements of the Felician heritage found in the *Constitutions* of the Congregation: "Dedicated to the Immaculate Heart of Mary, we honor her as Mother and Lady of our Congregation. We experience a loving communion with her Son, and through her, bring his redemptive healing to a suffering humanity. We look to Mary, our model of faith, for constant inspiration and guidance" (*Constitutions* I, 36). In virtue of each sister's consecration to Mary, the name of Mary is included as part of the religious name of each sister (*cf. Constitutions* I, 39).

By rendering homage to Mary and spreading devotion to her, the Felician Congregation strives to realize the teachings of Vatican Council II. In Chapter 8 of the *Dogmatic Constitution on the Church (Lumen gentium)*, dedicated specifically to the Mother of God, the Council Fathers remind us about the bond between the devotion to Mary and fidelity to Christ: "While the Mother is honored, the Son is rightly known, loved and glorified and his commandments are observed" (LG 66). That is why the Council "admonishes all the sons of the Church that the cult, especially the liturgical cult, of the Blessed Virgin Mary, be generously fostered, and that the practices and exercises of devotion towards her, recommended by the teaching authority of the Church in the course of the centuries, be highly esteemed and [. . .] be religiously observed" (LG 67).

The Council directs its teaching not only to religious sisters but to all of its sons and daughters. We all are called to render proper veneration, free of false exaggeration, to the Mother of God in accord with the teaching authority of the Church. She is the sign of true hope and comfort for the pilgrim People of God (*cf.* LG 68).

PRAYER

Blessed Mary Angela, Foundress of the Congregation of the Felician Sisters
   – pray for us.
Loyal servant of the Immaculate Heart of Mary
   – pray for us
Given to penance for the sins of neighbor and the world
   – pray for us.

O Mary, our Mother! Remember that we are yours; guard and protect us as your only possession!

O Mary, you are our Mother and our Superior. Rule over us and guide us. Preserve us and protect us from the enemies of the soul and body. Sanctify us. Obtain for us [. . .] perseverance in the service of your Son, and finally life everlasting [. . .].

I commend to you my soul so that it will not perish forever. O Mary, I am yours, and all that I possess belongs to you (SW III, 24).

XIII

LOVE OF COUNTRY

Give aid to all without exception; your vocation obliges you not to exclude anyone, for everybody is our neighbor. I know I need not encourage you to self-giving for you will not neglect anything, nor will you think of yourself, but only of the glory of God, of the common good, and that your aim will be the salvation of souls which will be your greatest concern, and that you will not get involved in other matters, being mindful of your calling and your position (SW I, 112).

The above-cited fragment is taken from the letter of Mary Angela to Sister Mary Hedwig. It was probably written in February or March of 1863, after the January uprising. In it Mother encourages the sisters to give aid to the wounded in the battlefields of the insurrection, but also cautions them against involvement in political affairs. This was to be understood because it would only trigger retaliation from the oppressors upon the fledgling Congregation.

The work of the sisters in teaching the basics of reading and writing in their native tongue and transmitting the faith in their language was a valuable service to their county. By conducting the Centers the sisters strengthened the bonds of ethnicity for all who availed themselves of their services. And, indeed, the activities of the Centers contributed to the preservation of the language and culture of the Polish nation.

The ardor which flamed the insurgency of 22 January 1863 was attributed to the immense love for their maltreated and tyrannized country. Her noblest sons sacrificed their lives for her very existence. The defeat of the uprising was an exceptionally sorrowful blow for all who loved Poland and the Church. Those who did not perish in the uprising became the victims of repression, torture, exile to Siberia, and death sentences. This same deep sorrow must have also transfixed the hearts of Mother Mary Angela and her sisters, who spared no efforts those days in bringing aid and relief to the victims of all the numerous catastrophes. The sisters hastened to help as if they had a premonition that time was running out.

In Warszawa, at their Central House, the sisters conducted an orphanage and a home for the care of the elderly and the disabled, and offered catechetical instruction. During the January uprising they organized a forty-bed so-called "lazaret" where they tended the wounded insurgents. In one of the letters to Sister Mary Hedwig, Mother Angela encouraged the sisters to care for the wounded, to bind not only their physical wounds but, above all, to care for their spiritual needs (*cf.* SW I, 75, 119). Sister Hedwig Sliwinska was at that time in charge of the sisters working in the field hospitals which were organized at the sites where, until then, they had conducted the Centers. This was in Kielce, in Miechow, and in the surrounding area where many of the battles had been fought. The sphere of Mother Mary Angela's various endeavors and activities at that time is a notable witness of her love for Poland, as expressed in coming to the aid of the wounded insurgents and in praying for the country.

Unfortunately, the very nature of these activities antagonized the enemies of the Polish nation and of the Catholic Church. The exceptionally social and patriotic character of the apostolic service conducted by Mother and her sisters led to the suppression of not only the first active-contemplative Congregation but also, at that time, the largest Congregation in the Kingdom of Poland. It became a victim of the repression by the invading powers.

At the end of December in 1864, the Congregation was disbanded by the Czar's edict which also forced the sisters to remove their habits and return to their homes (*cf.* SW I, 16). This was a stunning blow not only to Mother Foundress, but also to those whom the sisters helped—those whom they taught in the Centers to read, write, and pray in their native language. By the suppression of the religious orders in the Kingdom of Poland, the oppressor aimed to weaken the influence of the Catholic Church and through it also Polishness.

The religious orders served their country not only by bringing relief to indigent persons, but also through their prayers and their living witness to the faith. Mother Mary Angela was very disturbed by the events preceding the January uprising. She prayed fervently for God's mercy upon the nation and urged her sisters to do the same. In 1861 she wrote to Father Honorat that the sisters alternated day and night at prayer (*cf.* SW II/1,107). Despite all this intensive prayer, a sense of menace still hung over them but this only energized them to pray even more. In another letter written after the profanation of the churches in Warszawa, she described the state of her soul regarding the situation in their country and wrote that there is nothing left but our total reliance on prayer. (*cf.* SW II/1, 112).

Mother Mary Angela believed in the power of prayer, especially through the intercession of the Blessed Mother. She obtained everything through the recitation of the rosary in common (*cf.* SW III, 86; II/1, 270; II/2, 277). She was convinced that through the recitation of the Office of the Immaculate Conception in common they could obtain even more graces. That is why she desired that "this devotion be offered in the intentions of our country" (SW II/1, 114).

The attitude of the Felician Sisters and other religious communities, as regards the retaliation against the Church by the oppressors, undoubtedly fortified those who at that time suffered all types of suffering for their country. Prayer, trust in the Providence of God, and fidelity to moral principles helped to maintain a balance of spirit among the laity.

In speaking of Mother Mary Angela's relationship to her country, one cannot overlook her concern for the emigrants. Persecution in the country and abject poverty forced many to seek food and freedom across the ocean. In 1874, in response to an invitation of Father Joseph Dabrowski, Mother Mary Magdalena, the superior general, sent five sisters to the United States. Mother Foundress gave them her blessing for the trip. They undertook a religious-ethnic mission among the Polish emigrants. The sisters strengthened them in the faith while at the same time guarding them against the loss of their ethnicity. In a short time the Congregation began growing because of numerous vocations from among the local young women. Its rapid growth testifies to the fact that there was a great need for the presence of the sisters.

A beautiful example of Mother Mary Angela's love for Poland was her concern about the affairs of her country and the measure of help she was able to provide as a religious. Love of country, as befits one's state of life, vocation, or undertakings, is a duty of every citizen. This responsibility is addressed by the fourth commandment. The *Catechism* reminds us of the duties of citizens toward their country (*cf.* CCC 2199).

The *Catechism* links the obligations to one's country to the fatherhood of God in regard to all people. Every person is not only an individual within the human family, but also always a someone, a person who deserves respect as one who comes from God and is the object of his paternal love. Hence, we should regard our fellow citizens as sons and daughters of our country (*cf.* CCC 2212).

Further, the *Catechism* reminds us that the "love and service of one's country follows from the duty of gratitude and belongs to the order of charity" (CCC 2239). The love of one's country also signifies our co-responsibility for the common good. Our country is the common good and that is why we should be concerned that those who guard this good, or ought to guard it, should fulfill their obligation conscientiously. St. Paul teaches us about this issue: "Pay to all of them their dues [. . .], respect to whom respect is due, honor to whom honor is due" (Rom 13:7; CCC 2240).

The example of the love of country left to us by Mother Mary Angela remains continually actual. Moreover, in our times we do need the witness of faith, trust in God's Providence, and prayer for all involved in public affairs. Everyone who really loves his neighbor ought not to shirk consideration and interest in the common good, especially when there is some danger from evils, such as corruption, injustice, or self-seeking interests which become a detriment to the common good. The common good is also the authority of persons exercising public office, both in the Church and in the government. Hence, concern for their good name is a duty of every Christian, in conformity with the cited teaching of St. Paul.

PRAYER

Peace and justice for our country
– obtain for us, Mary Angela.
Apostolic zeal
– obtain for us, Mary Angela.
That we may raise our children and youth in the Christian spirit
– pray for us, Mary Angela.

O Holy Spirit, pour down your divine gifts on those who direct the fate of our country and upon the whole nation, that listening to your inspiration we may live according to the law of God in our private and public lives (Modl. 57).

O Mary of Jasna Gora, you who reign for so many centuries over Poland and her people; you who are a special Patroness and Foundress of our humble Congregation, have mercy on me and cure me of this sickness, in which I cry out over my sins (SW III, 22).

XIV

TRUST IN THE PROVIDENCE OF GOD

God is our Father and that is why he tells us to call him that in prayer. What should we fear having such a Father without whose will even one hair will not fall? It is surprising, that having such a Father, we could worry about anything else but that we should love him perfectly and serve him faithfully. Christ gave his apostles this question: "When I sent you on mission without purse or traveling bag or sandals were you in need of anything?" They replied: "Not a thing" (Lk 22:35). You too, remind yourself of your time of affliction when you did not have much confidence in God, did you perish? You will reply: "No." Why do you not have the courage to stand up to all your difficulties? God has not thus far abandoned you. Why should he now abandon you when you trust him more now than you ever did before? (SW III, 122).

Concern about worldly needs always absorbed and continues to absorb most of the attention of almost every individual. It appears that material wealth is able to assure human beings of happiness and long life. It is about this mental attitude that the Lord warns us in the parable of the sower whose field yielded an abundant crop (*cf.* Lk 12:16–21). In his Sermon on the Mount, he also cautions us against useless anxieties about life, food, and clothing: "The unbelievers are always running after these things. Your heavenly Father knows all that you need. Seek first his kingship over you" (Mt 6:32).

Mother Mary Angela believed these words completely. Her faith was rewarded and, beyond all doubt, she experienced them in reality. She witnessed this very clearly especially in the beginnings of the organization of her *Institute*.

In a letter to Father Honorat she describes the magnanimity of God's Providence. At the time when she was gathering a few women and several children, she gave them shelter and taught them what was essential. She made no attempts to solicit funds. Yet the people brought supplies in such abundance that it was sufficient to upkeep the *Institute*. This led her to this conclusion: "I do not know whether God was pleased with my intention, or whether he wanted to reward my faith, but he blessed my work in a special way. As more and more persons joined us, material resources increased likewise" (SW II/1, 16).

It is undeniable that this project pleased God. Today we have no doubt that it came from his inspiration because actually it is he who, in his concern about the poorest, manifests his love to them through the goodness of people.

Her faith in God's Providence was frequently put to the test. One such time of trial, for instance, occurred when, after the enfranchisement of the peasants, the landlords refused to support the sisters at the Centers. When the Margrave Wielopolski refused material assistance, Mother encouraged Sister Mary Hedwig not to lose confidence in God's protection and to model herself on the example of St. Francis.

"It would be unworthy of any Christian to fear to trust in Divine Providence"—she wrote—"but for a daughter of St. Francis it would be disgraceful. I hope, my dearest, that you will use this occasion to show that you understand the spirit of our Order. I lack words to tell you what gladness fills my heart as I write this to you, when I stop to consider your future so lofty, so glorious, and so rich in merit. I am positive that all this will work out not to the detriment of your soul but rather to the elevation of your spirit" (SW I, 139).

Mother Foundress was never disappointed in the trust she placed in the Providence of God. Thanks to her confidence, we can rest assured that anyone who completely depends upon God never needs to be concerned about the future. Such is also the point of view as taught by St. Peter: "Cast all your cares on him because he cares for you" (1 Pt 5:7). Would it be possible that the good God could forget about a person whose concern is whatever relates to God?

Totally in love with St. Francis of Assisi, Mother Foundress, desired most ardently to imitate his poverty and to permeate her Congregation with this spirit. She exhorted her spiritual daughters to continually keep their eyes fixed on his example. She suggested to Sister Mary Hedwig that in her work with the peasants, she should not set any conditions, but accept whatever they propose in the matter of upkeep for the sisters. "You will rejoice"—she wrote to her—"in imitating the poverty of Jesus and our Holy Father Francis, living like the birds that rely on the Providence of God. Then truly you can call yourselves daughters of the poor Francis" (SW I, 138).

In this experience and example of Mother Mary Angela, we should note that, even though she was totally dependent on God, she herself did not remain idle. Trusting in God's care for us does not imply a passive expectancy of "manna from heaven." Mother Foundress knew that cooperative efforts must always be part of the total reliance on God's Providence. St. Paul speaks of this: "We know that God makes all things work together for the good of those who love him, who have been called according to his decree" (Rom 8:28; cf. Mk 16:20). The empowering love of God renders it possible that a person can bear all sorts of suffering and yet not allow for any separation from that love (cf. Rom 8:31–39). In this way God enlightens us to understand that the Providence of God will not necessarily keep a person free from suffering (*cf.* Mt 10:29–31). The most eloquent testimony of this is the crucified Jesus in his agony as he felt abandoned by God (*cf.* Mt 27:46). Faithfully following Christ, Mary Angela never doubted the Providence of God, even in the midst of her greatest sufferings during the period of her mystical night of the soul.

At one time, it was quite frequently customary to interpret the Providence of God as God's reign over the world. Yet this "reign of God" is not discharged peremptorily like, for example, those laws of a country which of themselves bar any debate or questioning. God's Providence speaks of God's love for his creatures. John Paul II reminds us of this when, in accord with the *Book of Wisdom* (*cf.* Wis 7:22), he gives meaning to God's love: "God himself loves and cares, in the most literal and basic sense, for all creation" (*Veritatis Splendor*, 43). From this it follows that God's Providence does not force any free being to act or not to act. In the light of this teaching we see that God's Providence not only does not deprive his creatures of freedom but, on the contrary, it protects this freedom. This is also a manifestation of God's wisdom (*cf.* Wis 8:1).

In this providential care so full of love God reveals his laws, but expects from his creatures their voluntary obedience and consequent cooperation. That is why the Church teaches us to cooperate with God's Providence and guides us to share in it. Thanks to this, a person can collaborate in the accomplishment of a plan of God. In the *Catechism of the Catholic Church* we read that the Creator gives his creatures the dignity of acting on their own (*cf.* CCC 306). Thus it is that God entrusted to human beings the care of the earth by giving them dominion over it and by making it subject to them (*cf.* Gn 1:26–28). By being a participant in God's Providence we complete the work of creation (*cf.* CCC 307). The teaching of the *Catechism* rests on the words: "It is God who, in his good will toward you, begets in you any measure of desire or achievement" (Phil 2:13; CCC 308). The significance of this teaching then clearly indicates that God does not "rule" the world in a domineering or despotic fashion, but he entrusts to us the coresponsibility for ourselves and the world surrounding us. Thus he heightens the worth of our free will.

The works of Mother Angela, if placed in the above context, are examples of cooperation with the Providence of God. Her concern for the orphans and people in need was nothing less than the realization of God's concern for them. For these poor she was a person sent by the Providence of God to bind their wounds (*cf.* Is 61:1). The fulfillment of the commandment of love towards our neighbor is a sharing in the Providence of God. It is a summons to all Christians not only to expect the care of God's Providence, but also to assume responsibility in their own environment to become instruments actively engaged with the Providence of God. Shirking your responsibility in regard to the poverty in your surroundings would be casting it off unto others.

PRAYER

Blessed Mary Angela, whom God tested through the experience of the dark night of the soul
   – pray for us.
Blessed Mary Angela, who embraced the affairs of the Church in prayer, penance, and sacrifice
   – pray for us.
Blessed Mary Angela, who attained the glory of the altar through the cross and adversity
   – pray for us.

Eternal Father, I offer you the Most Sacred Heart of your Beloved Son, in thanksgiving for all the graces you have bestowed upon us, especially for the Most

Blessed Sacrament, for the Immaculate Conception of the Most Blessed Virgin Mary, and for the preservation and approbation of our Congregation (SW III, 25).

XV

DARKNESS GIVES WAY TO LIGHT

At present my life has changed as to the circumstances, disposition, variety of temptations which assail me, failures and evil tendencies of which I earlier considered myself incapable, and much interior confusion, so much so, that my soul seems to experience the unrest of the damned. Everything torments me [. . .].

It appears to me that my task is to keep silent, to suffer and endure things as they happen as long as Jesus will grant me the needed strength to bear it all [. . .].

I have much pain in my head and my ears and I think that I shall lose my mind since I do not have even a moment's relief. I do not desire any direction or spiritual help; I must only await the mercy of God to perform a miracle for me (SW II/1, 255–258).

This fragment of a letter of 21 August 1873 to Father Honorat testifies to the most painful dark night of the soul experienced by Mary Angela. It was a strange accumulation of suffering: a serious illness in the years of 1872–1873; the imposed necessity to remove oneself into the shadows; the intensity of interior suffering; and the onslaught of hardships and doubts. In her pursuit of holiness, this was undoubtedly an exceptional phase, a time of intensive spiritual maturation, the fruit of which was a miracle. It was a miracle of perseverance in fidelity, of surrender to God's will, and of heroic faithfulness and trust. This miracle endured for 26 years—to her death on 10 October 1899! This miracle was the lived reality of the cooperation of the free will of an individual with the grace of God.

However, the world was not to be made aware of this miracle for many years. The funeral services were held on 12 October 1899. Most Reverend John Puzyna presided over the funeral with the participation of numerous clergy and faithful. The body of the beloved Mother Foundress was interred in a chapel of the church which, through her efforts, had been built for the Congregation of the Felician Sisters in Krakow on Smolensk Street. The sisters received special permission from the Governor of Galicja to bury her in this chapel. Because of this arrangement, the mortal remains of Mother Angela were always near to her spiritual daughters. Convinced of the heroic virtues of their Foundress, the sisters frequently prayed at her grave for the grace of her beatification.

Those who knew Mother Mary Angela personally were aware of the extraordinary sanctity of her life. She led an ordinary life in a truly heroic manner. Many of the laity were convinced of her holiness. One of them, Countess Gabriela (Brezow) Wrotnowska, incensed by errors in the obituary of Mary Angela which was published in the *Church Newspaper* in Lwow on 28 December 1899, wrote a letter to the superior general of the Congregation of the Felician Sisters, Mother Mary Magdalena. In this letter she referred to Mother Foundress as "a saintly friend of my youth." She took it upon herself to correct the blunders in the obituary, specifically those regarding Mary Angela's "role and importance in the history of the Church of Poland as a Foundress of a Congregation." She concluded her letter with the information that she prays to Mary Angela daily "as to an instrument of God's great grace." The letter was written on 11 January 1900 (Archives). This is a powerful testimony about the life of Mother and remains a proof that she died in the opinion of holiness.

Shortly after the death of Mary Angela the Felician Sisters began to receive information about graces obtained through her intercession. Consequently as early as 1935, Mother Mary Pia, the superior general, began the preliminary preparations for the process of beatification. She received permission from His Eminence, Adam Cardinal Sapieha, Archbishop of Krakow, to print holy cards with a prayer for the beatification of Mother Mary Angela. The sisters began to gather materials required for the process. Unfortunately, World War II intervened and all these plans were thwarted. However, immediately after the war, in 1947, Mother Mary Simplicita, the then superior general, requested permission from the Archbishop to reopen the process. The Diocesan Informational Process began on 29 October 1949. His Eminence Adam Cardinal Sapieha oversaw the proceedings and, at the closing on 12 January 1951, signed the *Acts of the Process* which were submitted to the Holy See.

On 20 October 1967 the Apostolic Process opened in Krakow. His Eminence Karol Cardinal Wojtyla, who frequently visited the church of the Felician Sisters to pray before the exposed Blessed Sacrament, was in charge of the proceedings. This process came to a close with great solemnity on 23 June 1969 and the *Acts* were presented to the Apostolic See. Further sessions of the process in Rome began on 19 September 1969 and were closed on 2 April 1982 with a decree issued by the *Congregation for the Causes of the Saints* confirming the heroicity of the virtues of Mother Mary Angela.

This ended the first stage in the process of beatification whose aim was, as in all such cases of these processes, a verification of public opinion about the sanctity of the candidate for the altar. This is the extent of what the Church can announce at this stage of the process. Advancement to the second step follows only after the Church receives a sign from God, and this sign is a miracle wrought by God through the intercession of the candidate for the altar.

Mother Mary Angela obtained just such a sign from God, as a response to the prayers of certain individuals. This was the alleged miraculous healing of a Lillian Halasinski of the Diocese of Buffalo, New York in the United States of America. The authenticity of the alleged miracle was investigated in a separate process in the Diocese of Buffalo under the direction of the Most Reverend Edward Head in the years 1984–1986. The documents sent to the Apostolic See were then studied. On 11 August 1992, the decree of the *Congregation for the Causes of the Saints*, which acknowledged the miraculous healing through the intercession of Mary Angela, was read in the presence of the Holy Father John Paul II. Shortly after this, the date for the beatification of the Foundress of the Felician Sisters was determined.

The long awaited day in which the darkness finally gave way to light arrived on 18 April 1993. On this day Pope John Paul II publicly announced to the world the sanctity of life and heroicity of the virtues of Mother Mary Angela and included her in the company of the beatified. This is what he said about her then:

"Christ led Mother Angela by a truly exceptional path, causing her to share intimately in the mystery of the cross. He formed her spirit by means of numerous sufferings, which she accepted with faith and a truly heroic submission to his will: in seclusion and in solitude, in a long and trying illness, and in the dark night of the soul.

"Her greatest desire was to become a 'victim of love'. And she always understood love as a free gift of herself. 'Loving means giving. Giving everything that love asks for. Giving immediately, without regrets, with joy, and wanting even more to be asked of us.'

These are her own words in which she summed up the whole program of her life.

"She was able to kindle the same love in the hearts of the sisters of her Congregation. This love constitutes the ever living leaven of the works by which the communities of Felician Sisters serve the Church in Poland and beyond its borders" (*L'Osservatore Romano*. English Edition, 1267:1993, 1).

To this very day Mother Mary Angela ignites this love not only in the hearts of the sisters, but also in the hearts of many others. Many persons visit at her altar in Krakow and through her intercession pray to God for spiritual and physical healing. Each month numerous written appeals are left at her altar. Also, many notes of gratitude are deposited there, proving that the requests were answered. Because she herself suffered so much, Blessed Mary Angela Truszkowska is the patroness of the sick. She is able to intercede for many graces especially for the sick and suffering. It is not surprising then, that even at the time when Archbishop Wojtyla was still in Krakow, pastoral ministry of the sick and a clinic was established near her church, and is still active today. It is before the reliquary of her mortal remains in her church that the medical doctors of Metropolitan Krakow pray to deepen their love for the sick they serve.

Faithful to the charism of their Foundress and imitating her love, the Felician Sisters serve the Church of Poland and abroad. In 1997 there were 2,408 sisters in perpetual vows housed in 298 filial homes. At present the sisters in Poland conduct schools and pre-schools, catechize children and youth, conduct homes for exceptional children, minister to persons with terminal diseases in private homes and institutions, and sponsor pastoral ministry camps for the youth. They also serve in many capacities in parishes: they are organists, sacristans, and work in parish offices; and they assist in the pastoral ministry to the sick and homebound. In addition they conduct "kitchens" for needy students, senior citizens, and social security recipients.

In the United States of America, where the Felician Sisters are more numerous than in Poland, the sisters contributed to the development of the parish school system in the nineteenth century to satisfy the needs of Polish immigrant children. Today they continue work in parish elementary and high schools. They conduct day care centers, private high schools, colleges and a university, homes for exceptional children, hospitals, clinics, nursing homes, adult day care centers, residences for senior citizens and senior clergy, and hospice care. They also conduct retreats and administer retreat centers.

In Canada and Brasil they teach in kindergartens, in elementary and secondary education, and in adult education programs. They catechize and are involved in parish pastoral ministry and hospital chaplaincy programs; they minister to the elderly, to the needy, and to youth; and they serve in social action programs of the local Church.

Felician Sisters from both the Polish and American Provinces also serve in other countries. The sisters in Mexico catechize and evangelize. Sisters in Italy sponsor a program for feeding the poor and needy. In France the sisters do parish work and teach catechism to the young. The sisters in England minister in an assisted living home for the elderly, most of whom are of Polish heritage. In Kenya, sisters from Poland and the United States, together with native Felician Sisters, teach in day care centers and elementary schools, and are involved in hospital ministry. In Estonia and the Ukraine, the ministry is restricted to catechizing and ministry in Polish parishes. Faithful to the motto of their beloved Mother Foundress: "All through the Heart of Mary in honor of the Most Blessed

Sacrament," the Felician Sisters dedicate their total apostolic service to God.

The needs of the Church are numerous and, to fulfill them, the Congregation needs many Holy Spirit-motivated vocations. The sisters pray for this and by their life and witness they strive to attract young women to follow in the footsteps of their Mother Foundress. Though the contemporary mentality is not favorably disposed towards vocations to religious life, some young women still choose to follow this way of life. At present, however, there is a tremendous need for intensive prayer in this intention for ever increasing numbers of dedicated vocations through the intercession of Blessed Mary Angela.

LITANY OF
BLESSED MARY ANGELA TRUSZKOWSKA

*Foundress of the Congregation of Sisters
of St. Felix of Cantalice and Patroness of the Sick*

Lord, have mercy.
Christ, have mercy.
Lord, have mercy.
Christ, hear us.
Christ, graciously hear us.

God, the Father of Heaven, have mercy on us.
God, the Son, Redeemer of the world,[1]
God, the Holy Spirit,
Holy Trinity, one God,

Holy Mary, Mother of God
    and Lady of the Congregation, pray for us.

Blessed Mary Angela, Foundress of the Congregation
    of Felician Sisters, pray for us.
Prudent virgin, born in Poland,[2]
Gifted by the Creator with sensitivity
    to pain and human misery,
Guardian of children from the basements
    and attics of the poor,
Wise educator of youth,
Excellent spiritual director,
Apostle of truth and evangelical love,
Admirable example
    of Franciscan goodness and compassion,
Ardent venerator of the Mercy of God,
Zealous adorer of the Blessed Sacrament,
Loyal servant of the Immaculate Heart of Mary,
Peaceful and faithful in the most difficult situations,
Heroic in long-lasting suffering,
Given to penance for the sins
    of neighbor and the world,

---

[1] have mercy on us.
[2] pray for us.

Persevering in concern for the salvation of souls,[2]
Blessed Mary Angela, to whom God granted
the grace of understanding the redeeming value
of human suffering,
Blessed Mary Angela, who in suffering
praised and loved the will of God,
Blessed Mary Angela, whom God tested
through the experience of the dark night
of the soul,
Blessed Mary Angela, who embraced
the affairs of the Church in prayer,
penance, and sacrifice,
Blessed Mary Angela, who attained the glory
of the altar through the cross and adversity,

That we raise our children and youth
in the Christian spirit,[2]
That we may endure all burdens and sufferings
in union with Christ Crucified,
That through suffering we attain the Kingdom of God,
That through a life in accord with the Gospel
and our calling, we merit eternal life,

The grace to follow the Poor Christ,
obtain for us, Mary Angela.
A living faith,[3]
A pure love of God,
Perseverance in difficulties and sufferings,
A spirit of humility,
A ready submission to God's will,
A love of prayer,
Apostolic zeal,
A Christlike view of everyone and everything,
A generous spirit of dedication to the sick and needy,
A spirit of service and love for the Church,
Numerous and self-sacrificing vocations
to your Congregation,
Peace and justice for our country,

---

[2] pray for us.
[3] obtain for us, Mary Angela.

Lamb of God, you take away the sins of the world,
 spare us, O Lord!
Lamb of God, you take away the sins of the world,
 hear us, O Lord!
Lamb of God, you take away the sins of the world,
 have mercy on us!

V. Blessed are the merciful,
R. For they shall attain mercy.

Let us pray:

God, our Father, you graced Blessed Mary Angela with a living faith and a boundless love which she manifested in complete surrender to your divine will. By her prayers and witness may we strive to seek, to accept, and to fulfill your will in all circumstances of our lives.

Grant this through our Lord Jesus Christ, your Son who lives and reigns with you and the Holy Spirit, forever and ever. Amen.

PRAYER OF PETITION
THROUGH THE INTERCESSION
OF BLESSED MARY ANGELA

God, our Father, we praise and thank you for the gift of Blessed Mary Angela, who lived your will in faith and trust, and lived your love in service to others.

I pray, in confidence, that through her intercession you will grant me the favor which I request. I ask this through Christ our Lord. Amen.

EPILOGUE

The times in which we are living today demand great self-discipline in the life of a person seeking Christian perfection. In Blessed Mary Angela Truszkowska we find a splendid example of a life of total dedication to God through obedience to his will, lived in the spirit of poverty in imitation of St. Francis of Assisi.

Devotion to the Eucharist and to the Immaculate Heart of Mary are the characteristic elements of her Franciscan spirituality. This spirituality is expressed in the motto of her Congregation: "All through the Immaculate Heart of Mary in honor of the Most Blessed Sacrament".

Her wish to live an ordinary life in an extraordinary way merits special consideration. She did not yearn for any private revelations nor did she seek to be praised; she mortified herself even in her personal desires. Her only desire was to completely fulfill the will of God daily.

The second extraordinary feature of her quiet life was her perseverance in suffering, the source of which was twofold: her long incurable illness and her interior trials. These interior sufferings were intensified by her personal conviction that she did not know how to bear sufferings.

As a matter of fact, however, she possessed this competence in a heroic way. John Paul II said of her that Christ sculptured her soul with suffering. Because of her submission to the Divine Sculptor, a splendid masterpiece was created. In today's world, so imbued with the spirit of consumerism, she brilliantly shines as a model of perfect love of God and of neighbor.

Her love of the will of God, above all else, is a serious censure for our modern world, which so thoughtlessly disregards the commandments of God. Contempt for the laws of God is likewise contempt for human beings, generally the most vulnerable: children and the aged. There are many people today who, as they reflect on the sufferings of our times, have the audacity to accuse God of silence. Blessed Mary Angela, through her faithful fulfillment of God's will, has become an instrument of God's grace reflected in the tender love of the triune God for his people. Because of this she is an example for everyone who comes in contact with the richness of her legacy. Not only is she a model, but she is also our intercessor before God.

The interior life of Mother Mary Angela is extremely rich and deserves by far more attention. Unfortunately, it is not well known and, as yet, the indepth theological study of the mysticism of Mary Angela has not been realized. Reverend Valentino Macca, OCD, professor at the Teresianum in Rome and the author of the *Votum* on the mystical life of Mother, is convinced that such study is absolutely necessary in the interest of persons whom God may wish to lead to perfection in a similar way. Over and above this, Father noted that Mother's letters to her confessor are authentic and were written in the heat of a need which prompted them. They are indeed unique according to universal standards. Even before Mother's beatification, Father Macca expressed this opinion verbally to the Felician Sister involved in the process of beatification (Archives).

The example of the life of the Foundress of the Felician Sisters is for all times. Through the apostolic ministry of her spiritual daughters, she inspires many people to strive to live the will of God and to love God above all. At her beatification, Pope John Paul II said that she always understood love as a free gift of herself. Her own words were: "Loving means giving. Giving everything that love asks for. Giving immediately, without regret, with joy, and wanting even more to be asked of us".